ESCAPE BETWIXT TWO SUNS

Shawnee Books

Escape Betwixt Two Suns

A TRUE TALE OF THE UNDERGROUND RAILROAD IN ILLINOIS

Carol Pirtle

With a Foreword by Rodney O. Davis

SOUTHERN ILLINOIS UNIVERSITY PRESS

CARBONDALE & EDWARDSVILLE

Library of Congress Cataloging-in-Publication Data

Pirtle, Carol, 1938–
    Escape betwixt two suns : a true tale of the
underground railroad in Illinois / Carol Pirtle ;
with a foreword by Rodney O. Davis.
    p. cm. — (Shawnee books)
    Includes bibliographical references and index.

    1. Underground railroad—Illinois—Randolph
County. 2. Underground railroad—Illinois—Knox
County. 3. Fugitive slaves—Illinois—History—19th
century. 4. Hayes, William, d. 1849. 5. Abolition-
ists—Illinois Biography. 6. Fugitive slaves—Illinois
Biography. 7. Randolph County (Ill.)—History—
19th century. 8. Knox County (Ill.)—History—19th
century. 9. Hayes, William, d. 1849—Trials,
litigation, etc. 10. Trials—Illinois—Knox County—
History—19th century. I. Title.
F547.R2P55 2000   99-41339
937.7'115—dc21   CIP
ISBN 0-8093-2300-1 (cloth : alk. paper)
ISBN 0-8093-2301-X (pbk. : alk. paper)

To my grandchildren,
Kylie, Kate, and Colynn Vacko,
Cole and Ally Hoffbauer,
and to those who will bless the future

May you grow to become
men and women of courage and conviction

Then Peter and the other apostles answered and said,
We ought to obey God rather than men.

—Acts 5:29

Guide us, O thou great Jehovah;
Save, oh, save our guilty land!
Though our foe is proud and mighty,
Bind him with thy powerful hand;
See he rages; see he rages,
Bind him with thy powerful hand.

Open thou the prison doors;
Bid the bondsman freely go;
Let thine arm, revealed in power,
Bear his cause triumphant through;
Strong Deliverer, strong Deliverer
Bear his cause triumphant through.

While he treads the wheel of slavery,
Bid his hopeless fears subside;
Bear him through oppression's current;
Land him safe on freedom's side.
Songs of praises, songs of praises
Freedom's friends will give to thee.

—Antislavery Hymn

CONTENTS

Contents

ILLUSTRATIONS

FOREWORD

S lave mother Susan Richardson's escape from Randolph County, Illinois, with her three children in August 1842 has been the basis of a tale rather well known among scholars of early Illinois history and the Underground Railroad. Especially has this been true in Knox County, where the fugitives found both immediate refuge and eventually profound disappointment. Equally well known has been the effort of Susan's professed master, Andrew Borders, to reclaim the escapees, an effort that was successful in the case of the children but not so with Sukey herself. The actions of Knox College administrators and trustees in Sukey's behalf have also been a matter of local pride, as has their suspected but hitherto undocumented larger involvement in the Underground Railroad.

By bringing the William Hayes letters to light and producing this work based on them, Carol Pirtle has greatly amplified this story, and in doing so she has earned the gratitude of all students of both early Illinois and the Underground Railroad. An episode once known mainly in a single county now has a much fuller, statewide dimension. A close look at both the operations and the risks of aiding black fugitives is revealed here, at a level of individual activity that has long been, for rather obvious reasons, essentially undivulged. William Hayes, the hitherto undocumented Underground Railroad operative who helped Sukey escape from Randolph County and apparently went north with her, was undoubtedly a more typical functionary in that slave liberation system than were such more flamboyant and well-publicized figures as Owen Lovejoy or John Cross. But the very nature of the enterprise has ensured that the stories of most of the individuals involved in helping slaves to freedom have remained untold. It was best for most of those who aided slave escapees to remain essentially anonymous. What is equally arresting about this volume and the sources on which it is based is the description here of activity at both ends of an Underground Railroad transaction: the escape of slaves from their owner, in this case the details of which were not previously known; the response of their owner; litigation initiated by both the owner and by supporters of the fugitives; and in this instance the escapees' partially successful guarantee of permanent freedom. The autobiographies of escaped slaves themselves are usually the principal sources for such details.

At the center of this tale are three figures: Susan Richardson, a Randolph County African American mother held to indenture under Illinois's vague statutes involving voluntary servitude; Andrew Borders, her professed master and the major landowner in the county; and William Hayes, a Randolph County farmer who aided her flight north. Susan's initiative in escaping with her children set the other events in train, and the outcome of her escape was both successful and tragic for her; her freedom and a measure of security were guaranteed, but those of her children were not. And hers was not one of the cases in which the very right of Illinoisans to hold slaves was tested in the courts; that had to come later, and her freedom remained in jeopardy until it did.

Borders professed to be the aggrieved custodian of his slaves. He took full advantage of the ambiguity of Illinois laws and their interpretation, and he had the further advantage of the sympathy of the sheriff of Knox County. And it is clear from this account that in spite of his turbulent pro-slavery record, his great material success was what he was best remembered for in Randolph County; it ensured that he was an object of veneration there. He may have sought civil rather than criminal prosecution of Hayes specifically to preclude his right to hold slaves in Illinois being brought into question in the courts.

Hayes, who we learn about here for the first time, is the most enigmatic figure of the three. Though he speaks very little in the correspondence on which this volume is based, we are able nonetheless to learn some things about him. He was orderly and a careful planner, speculative and ambitious, yet obviously principled. At the same time he was ingenuous, litigious, and, in some very important matters, imprudent. What motivated him to aid slave escapees is not clear, other than that his membership in the Reformed Presbyterian Church must have influenced him to believe that no one has a right to deprive another of liberty. Otherwise he does not tell us. His economic security as well as that of his family were at stake as a result of this involvement in the Underground Railroad. How to assess the intentions of one for whom material matters are not the main motives for action is always a mystery in America. Somehow Hayes avoided the litigation at the Knox County end of the transaction at issue in this volume, and he thus has remained essentially unknown until now. Yet his inability to hold his tongue ensured that what he apparently said to Sheriff Frans and Sally Newman in Knox County would be held against him when he himself was a defendant in southern Illinois. His pride in helping Sukey come north was manifest when he was in the North, yet he denied involvement in her escape when confronted in Randolph County. We need to be reminded that both Susan Richardson and William Hayes were perceived as outlaws in their time and that Andrew Borders was considered aggrieved and law-abiding, at least insofar as the appropriate laws were interpreted in the 1840s. And it is indicative of the long tenure of these prejudices that Hayes's descendants, though they preserved these letters, were also ashamed of him as a lawbreaker. That he and they saved these letters and preserved them for a century and a half is extraordinary, for though outlaws generally hide their tracks, William Hayes didn't hide his, and we, along with those he aided in their flight to freedom, are ultimately his beneficiaries.

Other individuals who figure in this volume deserve mention. The trial of William Hayes in Perry County involved Illinois luminaries for whom the issue of slavery, very much at the center of this lawsuit, would continue to affect their political careers. William H. Bissell and Gustave Koerner, attorneys for the slaveholding Borders, and Lyman Trumbull, who represented Hayes, were all allies in the Democratic party in the 1840s. But by 1856 all would be newly recruited Republican leaders in Illinois, avidly opposed to the Kansas-Nebraska Act, which would allow the extension of slavery into the territories, and calling for the restoration of the Missouri Compromise. All would become advisors and correspondents of Abraham Lincoln.

Nehemiah West is much less known than these three outside Knox County, but he was a founder of Galesburg and Knox College and a trustee of that institution in 1842. William Hayes's correspondence renders it obvious that West and others connected with Knox College were active participants in the Underground Railroad, thus ratifying previously unprovable local folklore. Yet, principled man that he was and dedicated to the anti-slavery cause as he was, West could not perjure himself in a legal deposition when asked how the fugitives had said that they had traveled to Knox County. It was West's testimony implicating Hayes before Borders's attorneys that was particularly damaging to William Hayes at his trial.

Hayes suffered financially as a result of this litigation, and he died intestate with his affairs in some disarray, leaving his family in a state of financial insecurity. But they were able to remain in Randolph County, as have many of his descendants. Those descendants' feelings of shame at their ancestor's role as a lawbreaker has evolved over the generations into one of pride, finally making it possible for his correspondence to be brought to light. And that in turn has enabled Ms. Pirtle to produce this graceful account. We may consider it long overdue.

Rodney O. Davis

ACKNOWLEDGMENTS

I could not have written a book that depends so heavily on research without the help of numerous people who scrambled to find answers to my questions. All were helpful and giving of their time and talents, and for this I am most grateful.

Of course, without the letters and the trial transcript, there would be no book. The Hayes family of Sparta cooperated fully in my effort to uncover the actions of their ancestor, William Hayes. Gladys Hayes, keeper of the family legacy, was an enthusiastic supporter from the beginning and answered any and all questions about the family. To her and to her late husband, Russel, I am very much indebted. In addition, Jim and Phyllis Hayes, who live in William's farmhouse in Flat Prairie, loaned the letters in their possession and rummaged in their attic to find even more. Perry Dickey of Bartlesville, Oklahoma, also a descendant of William Hayes, helped immensely with his genealogical work on the Hayes family.

No one took more time with me or answered my numerous questions with more patience than Dr. Rodney O. Davis, Szold Professor of History Emeritus and codirector of the Lincoln Studies Center at Knox College in Galesburg, Illinois. He encouraged my efforts from start to finish and provided me with prompt and accurate answers to the frequent questions I sent to Galesburg.

Despite his jam-packed schedule, Sparta lawyer Alan Farris never failed to return a phone call or meet with me in his office when I ran into the numerous difficulties I had comprehending the ins and outs of the legal system.

Mr. and Mrs. Jim Borders of Belleville, Illinois, were most gracious and helpful in sharing what they knew about their ancestor, Andrew

Borders, a man who achieved much during his life, but who also was a product of his time.

Many others contributed to my research, and to them I am most grateful. Tom Seals walked a creek bed with me by the light of the moon and unlocked the mysteries of the plat book; Rev. Ray Morton, pastor of the Sparta Reformed Presbyterian Church, Minnie Finley, Anna McIntyre, and Bob Finley shared Session records and information that helped me understand the beliefs of the Covenanters.

My heartfelt thanks go also to others who helped in big and small ways to make this book what it is. Paula Brickey took pictures of the Galway, New York, area so that I could "feel" the place from which William Hayes came; Larry and Debbie Bernardoni loaned me their "writer's get-away-on-wheels"; Dr. Carl Schlageter taught me about the symptoms of the "ague"; and my friends Linley Bartell, Patti Schlageter, Gloria Schobert, and Jan Seals let me talk on and on about William Hayes and his work. Patricia Harrelson and Joy Neal Kidney, my 1997 classmates at the University of Iowa Summer Writing Festival, read the first chapters of the book and contributed valuable suggestions.

To my husband Konnie goes an extra big kiss in payment for his patience and good humor on days when he ate slipshod meals and had to hunt for an ironed shirt.

There are not enough words to express how much support and encouragement my children, Lisa, Patrick, and Laura, gave me over the last nine years. And without the computer expertise of my son Patrick, I would still be floundering in a sea of unintelligible (to me) computerese. He is, without a doubt, the world's best teacher.

And, finally, I would never have had the courage to tackle a book without the love of learning instilled in me by my late father Fred A. Frede or the lifetime of support given by my mother June Frede Burgess. They brought me up in a home that valued education above all else and gave me the confidence to follow my dreams.

INTRODUCTION

In answer to your kind questions, Nathan Jones of Canton, is not a brother but a cousin. He is of the "true blue" sort of Abolitionists. The first slave that ever we knew of escaping from the "Puke" State [Missouri] came to us in Canton. That is one of the strong holds of Abolition. . . . You Dear Sir are to me an unknown friend, yet I believe you are a friend to the poor down trodden Slave. This is as good an introduction as I want from any man. My brother, our cause is a holy one. . . . Please to write me again, and let me know how the cause prospers there. . . . I am Sir your most humble brother in the cause of the Slaves.

—T. A. Jones to William Hayes,
Greenville Bond County, Illinois, February 27, 1843

I stopped breathing when I read those words. The message from T. A. Jones confirmed what I had been told: William Hayes, a small-time dairy farmer and some-time land speculator who lived on the Flat Prairie outside Columbus (now Sparta), Illinois, had indeed been active in the Underground Railroad long before the Civil War.

The letter from T. A. Jones was only one of more than two hundred belonging to James V. Hayes, William Hayes's great-great grandson. Guarded like family jewels, the cache of correspondence was stashed in a battered wooden box hidden beneath the stairwell of the farmhouse William Hayes had built sometime before 1840. When I learned of their existence in 1989, I was racing to meet a deadline for my first book—a history of Sparta, Illinois. The prospect of reading them so excited me that for one brief, crazy moment I considered chucking the history book to dive into them immediately. I soon regained my senses, and it would be another four months before I had the time and opportunity to trace the scrawled, spidery lines that told a tale of intrigue and mystery.

Because the letters had been largely unread for 150 years, I could only speculate on the family legend that described the story of William Hayes and his work in the Underground Railroad. Was it true that he helped five slaves escape to northern Illinois in the early 1840s? Was it true that the slave owner, Andrew Borders, sued him for aiding in the escape of his "property"? Was it true that the case eventually reached the Illinois State Supreme Court? Only by untangling the meaning from the sometimes indecipherable lines could I be sure of what was fact and what was fiction.

I spent six months transcribing the heap of letters tossed carelessly in the box. Since they were in sequential disarray, the stories they told were fragmented until I completed the transcription and placed them in chronological order. Only then could I follow the narrative thread of this ordinary nineteenth-century family whose lives were affected by the most burning issues of the day: Does anyone have the right to hold other people as property? Does the color of a person's skin determine his or her worth, intelligence, independence, or even the existence of an individual's soul? And do people have the right to break the laws of humanity to follow what they perceive as the laws of God?

Like other letters written before the Civil War, these had no envelopes. Rather, they were folded, then folded again, and sometimes yet again, until a blank section presented a smooth face on which to write an address. None of them contained stamps. Postage rates were marked, usually in pencil, in the upper-right-hand corner, and the rates varied from ten cents to twenty-five cents, depending on the distance the letter had to travel. Only the ones from major cities held postmarks. A few were marked "Free" in the upper-right corner. These are examples of the franking system used by postmasters of the day— men who received free postal service in exchange for their duties. The practice benefited not only them but also anyone to whom they wrote because the recipient, not the sender, paid the postage. Several carry no postage marks at all and were presumably hand carried by friends or relatives visiting the Hayes family.

Correspondence originating in southern Illinois bore a variety of return addresses—Bethel, Shannon's Store, Randolph County—but all referred to the Flat Prairie area located about two miles east of the present-day town of Sparta, then called Columbus. Bethel was the name of the Reformed Presbyterian Church to which William and Anna Hayes belonged; Shannon's Store was the post office located in Columbus.

The letters are in surprisingly good condition. Though stained and streaked with grime, only a few are torn or have missing sections. The paper remains supple, not brittle as one would expect. Most of them are legible to anyone who has the patience to decipher the intricate penmanship.

Since the letters were written by people who received only a rudimentary education, most have used "creative" capitalization, spelling, punctuation, and grammar. These departures from standard English usage made interpretation a challenge, and it sometimes took a great deal of imagination to untangle the meaning from the complex penmanship. As a rule, men seemed better educated than women and had a firmer grasp of the written word. Most women's letters displayed a frightening lack of education, but letters written by children indicated that instruction of the next generation was more thorough than for their parents. The letters quoted use the original spelling, punctuation, and capitalization unless revision was needed to clarify the meaning.

Among the cache of letters, I discovered a handwritten trial transcript of a suit brought by Andrew Borders against William Hayes in 1844. This forty-five page document held by Mr. and Mrs. James V. Hayes is the only record known to exist. The Perry County Courthouse in Pinckneyville, Illinois, has no extant account of the official court record.

I became so caught up in the story of Sukey and William Hayes that on the evening of August 31, 1992, exactly 150 years after Sukey's escape, I retraced what I believe to be the route she took as she and her children fled to the farmhouse owned by William Hayes. With only the light of the moon to guide my steps, I walked the narrow, nameless creek that flows back of the Borders property. I tripped on the rocks of the creek bed; I struggled up its steep banks, hauling myself hand over hand using only tangled roots and the saplings lining the bed; I learned firsthand how clear the night sky is in summer and how difficult it is to find a path using only "night eyes." I saw how bright the North Star shone, and I understood for the first time the words of the old slave song "Follow the Drinking Gourd."

I had no children to care for as I walked the creek; no one was pursuing me; I had no fear of being caught. And yet, by this experience, pallid when compared to the circumstances when Sukey had done it 150 years before, I came to understand the courage it took for a young mother to flee the only home she had ever known in an effort to find a better life for herself and for her young sons.

And as I read the words written to the white man who helped her on her journey to find that better life, I entered another time, another place, another world. Even now, when I reread the letters to find a quote or check a fact, I am flung back into that world—a world that is sometimes more real to me than my own. I laugh with these long-dead correspondents; I cry with them; I rejoice with them; and I came to love them as though they are *my* family or *my* friends.

Often since I discovered the letters, I have ridden my bicycle over back roads to Caledonia Cemetery to the graves of William and Anna Hayes. Though it may sound crazy, I talk to them regularly as I stand before the simple stones marking their final resting place. And I ask them questions: Why did you do it? How did you do it? Of course, no answers come to me, only a puff of breeze on a summer's day or a sharp blast of autumn air as summer turns to fall. I don't know what I expect, but visiting William brings me peace. I bring him flowers when they are blooming and wish I had known him personally.

Though many of the letters speak of the mundane facts of family and business, the most fascinating ones begin about 1840, when references to William Hayes's work in the Underground Railroad began to appear. No details of this case have been found, but it is apparent that his family, living in upstate New York, had been informed of his activities. His older brother James wrote:

Galway, New York April 9th, 1841

. . . I have heard you had trouble for helping the Blacks with a Ride[.] let me know about that too. I should think it would be

more pleasure and as much profit to wait on your own Family
and let the Concerns of others Especially the Blacks go to others
for help. I am opposed to Slavery but think free states better not
interfere with the Laws of the States Where Slavery Exists no
further than to exert a good moral influence. . . .

James Hayes

Not all family members shared his disapproval. Later that year,
Anna's half brother, Michael Johnston, wrote:

Albany
31 October 1841

. . . I must take this opportunity before I close this to express my
approbation of the course you have pursued in regard to the
slaves that providence cast in your way. . . .

Your affectionate brother

Michael Johnston

Real people speak from the pages of letters originally intended for
private eyes. Some wrote often; others appear a single time. All the correspondents offer tantalizing glimpses into their lives and the lives of
the people to whom they wrote—William and Anna Hayes. The story
they tell is a drama worthy of the stage.

ESCAPE BETWIXT TWO SUNS

I

Sukey

Susan Richardson, for such was "Aunt Sukey's" real name, was brought into the Territory of Illinois a few years before it was admitted into the Union as a State. Her master, Andrew Border[s], lived in Randolph county, where she was kept a slave until, as she told us, "she left betwixt two suns."

—*History of Knox County, Illinois,* 1878

A quarter moon hung low over Lively Prairie in Randolph County, Illinois, on Wednesday, August 31, 1842. Its light bathed the rolling prairie land surrounding the imposing farmhouse of Andrew Borders in light so bright that someone crossing the fields behind his home could have been seen by anyone glancing out his windows. On that night, when summer began turning toward fall, Sukey, a thirty-year-old slave woman belonging to Borders, prepared to bundle her three young sons, Jarrot, Anderson, and Harrison, for a late-night escape into the darkness that beckoned from the woods lining a nearby creek. The escape may have been planned, but it was more likely an impulsive act on her part, though one she had probably considered for some time.

Andrew Borders was notorious in the area for his inhumane treatment of his slaves—six of them at that time—so much so that their condition aroused "the sympathy of the whole neighborhood."[1] The year before, in 1841, Borders had severely beaten Sarah, a slave whom he purchased in 1825, for some minor infraction and injured her arm.[2] She escaped, leaving her daughter Hannah behind, and hid at the home of a Randolph County sympathizer, possibly Matthew Chambers, a thirty-year-old shoemaker.[3] Chambers was accused of "harboring" her on April 18, 1842. His case was not heard until April 26, 1843, when a jury found Chambers guilty and fined him twenty dollars.[4] Chambers appealed the case to the Illinois Supreme Court; the state court reversed the judgment in December 1843.[5]

Also in April of 1842, the Friends of Rational Liberty, a group of Randolph County abolitionists, sued Borders in Sarah's name for assault and battery and past wages. The chief issue in the suit was the effect of the Ordinance of 1787, since Sarah had been indentured before Illinois became a state.[6] Though Illinois was officially classified under Article IV of the Ordinance of 1787 as a free territory when Borders arrived, it historically had a lenient attitude toward slavery. The ordinance expressly condemned any involuntary servitude, but since slaves had been held by the French settlers since 1719 when Philippe François Renault "brought 500 negro slaves to Illinois, landing them at the site of the 'ancient village of St. Philip,'" the document permitted people to keep them.[7] These slaves, whom Renault had purchased in the West Indies, and their descendants made up the "original French slaves" of Illinois.[8] A petition was issued to Congress in 1802 seeking ten years of slave trade in the Illinois territory because the Ordinance of 1787 was "extremely prejudicial to their interest and welfare" and because it "prevented the country from populating."[9] In ensuing years, officials either ignored the practice of slavery or rationalized it on the grounds that it had always been permitted in the territory.

Andrew Borders won the suit the Friends had instigated in Sarah's behalf in the circuit court at Kaskaskia, but the case was appealed to the Illinois Supreme Court in order to challenge the legality of holding slaves in a free state. Before the Illinois Supreme Court reached a decision on Sarah's case, however, the other five slaves held by Borders fled.

An argument between one of Sukey's children, probably her oldest son, Jarrot, and those of the Borders family provided the impetus for Sukey to take action. In the ensuing squabble between the children, Sukey's child was beaten. Martha Borders demanded that Sukey also be punished, but her husband refused to do this because, supposedly, he was afraid that Sukey might run away. However, he granted permission for his wife to administer a punishment and offered to tie up Sukey for a beating. More importantly, he threatened to sell the young boys South. No doubt it was this last threat that determined Sukey's actions. Rather than face a whipping and the possibility of losing her sons, Sukey ran, taking her children and Sarah's daughter, Hannah, with her. Jarrot was about twelve years old; Anderson a toddler nearing four; and Harrison was only two.[10] Anderson and Harrison had been indentured on March 24, 1841. At that time, Anderson was listed as "two years and two months old"; Harrison was "six months old." Jarrot's indenture papers were drawn on September 3, 1839. His age was torn out of the official registry, but it is believed that he was ten or twelve at the time of the escape. The children were indentured to the age of twenty-one.[11]

Hannah was a young woman believed to be about nineteen or twenty. Reportedly, her indenture had expired the year before, but Borders had continued to hold her in bondage, and she had not been given her Certificate of Freedom.

Little is known about Sukey before she arrived in Randolph County, other than that she had been brought to Illinois from Georgia by Andrew Borders. According to the Registry of Negroes, Mulattoes &c, which was entered into the trial transcript, "Suky" was indentured to Borders on January 10, 1817. Her age is listed as "about 5 years old." She was indentured until the age of thirty-two. Sukey was thirty-one at the time of the escape.[12] Though it is not known how or where Borders acquired her, family legend says that Sukey originally belonged to Martha Borders, Andrew's wife, and he had acquired her as part of a dowry.

By 1830 Sukey had borne her first son, Jarrot, who is described in the trial transcript as a "mulatto."[13] Using this word to describe Sukey's oldest son leads to the speculation that perhaps Andrew Borders was his biological father. Though no proof of this is available, Southern masters routinely sexually violated their slaves, and it is possible that Borders was not an exception. His reluctance to beat her, though asked to by his wife Martha, may also indicate he looked on her with favor.

By 1842 Sukey was the mother of two more sons, Anderson and Harrison. The word "mulatto" is not ascribed to either child in the trial transcript, but, since Borders owned no male slaves, the paternity of their fathers is also open to speculation.

2

The Major

When Major Borders arrived in this County, he brought
with him four slaves. He treated them with humanity and
kindness, and, unlike some others, he did not sell them
South.

—*Illustrated Historical Atlas
of Randolph County,* 1875

Borders arrived in Randolph County on January 1, 1816, bringing
with him his wife, Martha, an infant daughter, Martha's mother,
Sarah Clark, and four slaves, among them Sukey. According to the
county atlas published in 1875, Borders treated his slaves with "great
humanity and kindness." Subsequent events prove that assertion to
be a lie. The slaves represented his only wealth at the time because,
after paying the expenses of the trip north, he had only fifty cents left
in his pocket.

Though Illinois was officially a "free" territory, all indentured servants, as slaves were called in Illinois, had to be registered in the Registry of Negroes, Mulattoes &c at the Randolph County Courthouse in
Kaskaskia, then the territorial capital. It took Borders some time to
comply with this requirement. Sukey wasn't registered until January
10, 1817, but it's doubtful that anyone pressured him on this
issue.[1] Indentured servitude was tolerated, even encouraged, in the
southern part of the state at the time.

The year 1816 may have been an appalling time to be homesteading
because reports indicate that bizarre weather conditions existed world-
wide. Though Illinois was so undeveloped that weather records are
nonexistent, contemporary newspaper accounts from eastern and

southern newspapers reported extensive abnormalities in the weather, especially during the summer months. Problems, though, had surfaced in late winter and early spring with widespread drought and unseasonably cold temperatures that destroyed crops and drove grain prices to astronomical levels. In June, instead of the usual warm weather, snow fell throughout the populated portions of the country, and temperatures reached a high of only 40 degrees. The low temperatures were followed by a killing frost that destroyed most vegetation. Damage was most severe in New England, but reports of similar occurrences came from southern and western states as well.[2] Cold weather, hard frosts, and prolonged drought were repeated in July and August, so much so that 1816 has been termed "the year without a summer" and "Eighteen hundred and froze to death."

Reports of the unusual weather in spots close to southern Illinois came from Missouri and Kentucky. On June 9 the *Little Rock Gazette* reported snowfall "up in the inches" from "Arkansa," then the southern county of the Missouri Territory.[3] On August 21 and 22, Washington, Kentucky, was hit by "a frost so severe, as in some instances to kill vines in exposed situations." It was followed by "considerable frost" on August 28 and 29.[4]

Such strange weather phenomena were reported in European newspapers as well, so it seems likely that southern Illinois was also affected by the weather peculiarities. The reasons for the extraordinary weather patterns that year are not known, though speculations abound. Some scientists attribute the odd weather to active volcanoes that produced dust, covering the sun all over the world; others credit sunspots and/or a decrease in ocean surface temperature.

Whatever the cause, the "year without a summer" produced great anxiety throughout the country as the specter of famine became more than a distant threat. Even Thomas Jefferson was concerned, as he noted the scarcity of crops when he wrote to his friend Albert Gallatin: "My anxieties on this subject are greater because I remember the deaths which the drought of 1755 in Virginia produced from the want of food."[5]

Reactions to the weather ranged from a surge toward religious revival as citizens begged God for relief from the cold and drought to an increase in westward expansion in those who wished to outrun the scourge that seemed to be overtaking the country. Settlers like the Borders family, who had spent that first winter tent-camping on a hillside west of present-day Sparta, probably survived by living on wild game and the numerous prairie chickens that lived on the county's prairies.[6] At the time, the nearest town of any size was Kaskaskia, the territorial capital of Illinois, located about twenty-five miles away.

Since the northeastern portion of Randolph County, where Borders chose to put down roots, was relatively uninhabited, that first year must have been lonely, as well as filled with deprivations. Settlers began drifting into the area, however, about 1820, when a group of Covenanter Presbyterians from North Carolina established a church in Eden, about six miles from where Andrew Borders set up his camp.

The first few years were busy and difficult ones for Borders because he had so little money. Land could be bought cheaply, but one had to have some hard cash to make a down payment. Unlike many of the Southerners who trickled into Randolph County, though, Borders was ambitious. He built a small cabin, spent a few years working for another man in a distillery, and, in January of 1818, exactly two years after his arrival, purchased a little over 134 acres of rolling prairie land.[7] Three years later, he managed to buy another 100 acres of land. Eventually he became the largest landowner in the area, owning thousands of acres of land in Randolph, Washington, and St. Clair counties.[8]

Besides breaking the prairie land and planting his first crops, Borders built the first gristmill in that section of the county, operating it by horsepower. During those years, too, he joined the middle branch of the Presbyterian Church (Union Church) and increased his family, eventually becoming the father of ten children and the master of several more slaves. Little by little, his hard work and ambition brought him wealth and power.

Andrew Borders came to the Illinois country bearing military titles: first "Major" and subsequently "Colonel." No national or state military archives can locate his name in their records, however, so the titles probably were affectations on his part, something Southerners often did.

Borders arrived in southern Illinois with little more than ambition and a dream for the future, and though he had chosen an area where residents were ostensibly "free," he could continue the practice of slavery with little or no interference from the local community. The Ordinance of 1787, which contained a clause prohibiting slavery northwest of the Ohio River, interfered very little with men like Borders because then-governor St. Clair decreed that the provision was intended only to prevent the introduction of *new* slaves into the territory. Existing slaveholders could retain their property. Governor Ninian Edwards advanced the notion in 1817 that the Ordinance of 1787 permitted the "voluntary" servitude of Negroes for "limited periods of service."[9]

One reason the 1787 Ordinance was not strictly interpreted was because so many Southerners bypassed Illinois in favor of Missouri, where slavery was legal. In order to qualify for statehood, Illinois needed to reach a population of sixty thousand people. By turning a blind eye to the slavery issue, Illinois could attract many more permanent settlers.

In 1819, one year after Illinois reached statehood, the Illinois legislature passed a group of laws known as the "Black Code"; these laws further protected slave owners and virtually assured the continuance of slavery in the state. According to the Black Code, men could be indentured until the age of thirty-five, women until they were thirty-two. Slaves could be brought into the area, but masters were required to register them at the respective county clerk offices within thirty days of arrival. This probably had been the custom prior to 1819, because Andrew Borders had registered Sukey and his other black slaves at the courthouse in Kaskaskia, though it took him more than a year to comply with the law.

Some stipulations in the Black Code seemed to be in the slaves' best interests. Masters were required to provide them with essential, though meager, clothing. Each slave was to receive "a coat, waistcoat, a pair of breeches, one pair of shoes, two pair of stockings, a hat, and a blanket." Good food and lodging were also deemed important.[10] Rarely were these requirements strictly enforced. Most masters treated their slaves in whatever ways they wished.

Nearly all regulations in the Black Code favored the white masters. Whipping of lazy and recalcitrant slaves was permitted, and those who tried to escape or refused to work were required to serve two days extra time for every idle or absent day. In addition, African Americans could not serve in the state militia, were denied bail when arrested, could not gather in "unlawful" assemblies, and could not leave their masters' property without a special pass. Twenty-five lashes in front of a justice was permitted if a slave was found ten miles from his or her home. The ultimate threat from the Black Code stipulated that any slave who refused to work after being brought into Illinois could be sold "down South" to the slave states.[11]

Even people who claimed to abhor slavery sometimes owned slaves. Christiana Tillson, in a memoir about life in early Illinois, justified the purchase of two slaves because "I could not think of having them sent off to the slave pens of New Orleans." Life with her family, where the slaves would be treated well, was, she thought, infinitely better than life in the slaveholding South. Tillson also had very practical reasons for keeping slaves: "[M]y kitchen labors were to be abated." Such rationalizations may have been prevalent with many reluctant slave owners in Illinois. Despite her excuses for owning slaves, Tillson admitted that "work was made lighter, but conscience not quite easy."[12]

In 1824 the question of slavery in Illinois came to a head with a constitutional election that would decide either to permit or deny slavery in the new state. The Southern view of slavery held fast in Randolph County, and it was one of a handful that voted in favor of permitting slavery. Voters elsewhere in the state, however, voted against slavery, thus turning the tide against the pro-slavery faction that dominated Randolph County. The election held on August 1, 1824, resulted in 4,972 votes being cast for slavery; 6,640 voted against it.[13] The result of the election was that slaveholding in Illinois was banned forever.

However, this election did little to change things on the Borders farm. Andrew Borders continued to hold his slaves, despite the law, though in doing so he increasingly became the target of his antislavery neighbors.

Apparently, he was not the only Randolph County resident who continued to hold slaves. As late as 1840, the local newspaper, the *Sparta Democrat,* carried advertisements for escaped slaves, though judging from the one given below, slaves weren't valued as highly as horses, which were advertised in the same period with a five-dollar reward.[14]

ONE CENT REWARD

Runaway from subscriber, . . . an indented boy by the name of Leonard Huff. Said boy is 16 years old, 5'1" in height and has a flat foot. He absconded on the 17th ult. I will give the above reward and no thanks to any one who will fetch said boy back, and hereby forewarn all persons from harboring or trusting him, as I will pay no debts of his contracting.

Nathan Fields[15]

Even though slavery had once and for all been abolished in Illinois, pro-slavery advocates were elected to state offices. Shadrach Bond, first governor of Illinois, owned seven male slaves and six female slaves in 1825; the lieutenant governor, Pierre Menard, owned seven male and five female slaves at the same time.[16] Many other state officials were passionately pro-slavery. In 1825 Elias Kent Kane, Illinois's first secretary of state, owned two male slaves and three female slaves, among them Sarah and Hannah, whom he later sold to Andrew Borders.[17] All these state officials were residents of Randolph County.

Before 1840, three classes of African Americans lived in Illinois, none of whom had any legal status: indentured servants, French slaves, and free "colored" people. All were ostracized and denied citizenship or social recognition. Even free blacks did not have the right to own property, vote, serve as witnesses, hold public office, or even go to school. Few avenues for employment were open to them because many trades refused to employ blacks. They could not be forced into slavery as long as they owned a precious Certificate of Freedom, but this seems to be the only advantage free African Americans had.

The majority of whites preferred a "head in the sand" approach to the subject of slavery. Prevailing thought held that if the subject was ignored, maybe it would go away. Southerners like Borders, of course, were loath to give up their "property" and maintained a decidedly pro-slavery stance in defiance of the law. Other whites, many of them also from the South, held decidedly abolitionist views of slavery. Increasingly, as the years progressed toward the 1840s, they agitated for their cause through the antislavery societies that began forming in Illinois about 1838.

Most citizens in Randolph County held an opinion regarding slavery, and many of them were quite vocal about it. Some were involved in forming the Randolph County Anti-Slavery Society sometime in the late 1830s. This group, which met at the Bethel Church in Eden, became quite active in their opposition to slavery.

3

A Divided County

We publish today a statement by a committee on behalf
of an anti-slavery society of this county. An apology is
unnecessary; it is an act of sheer justice to let every society
explain their own views, especially when they are buffeted
on all sides.

—*The Sparta Herald,* March 20, 1840

The local paper rarely carried reports of abolitionist activities in
Randolph County, but it made an exception early in 1840. Even
then, a preamble to a statement by the Anti-Slavery Society was pref-
aced with a paragraph defending the reasons why the newspaper
printed a letter that might be inflammatory to its readership.

The editor had good reason to be wary of public opinion. Just three
years before, Elijah Lovejoy, editor of the *Alton Observer* and an outspoken abolitionist, was murdered while trying to protect his presses
from an angry mob of pro-slavery advocates.[1] One slaveholder said, in
regard to Lovejoy's death, "I am glad he is dead—he ought to die,"
but he regretted his murder because "every drop of Lovejoy's blood
will spring up a full grown abolitionist."[2] Feelings on both sides of
the slavery question still ran high in southern Illinois.

Abolitionists were generally thought to be wild-eyed fanatics,
and sometimes public sentiment could be very antagonistic. No-
where was this more prevalent than in Randolph County, where two
types of settlers made their homes. The editor of the *Sparta Herald*
realized this when he wrote the preface to a letter from the Anti-
Slavery Society:

> So far as our knowledge extends, abolitionists, so called, are equal to any other class of the community for morality and intelligence and should not be condemned without a hearing. We have heretofore avoided this exciting controversy, and it is not our intention now to engage in it; yet upon the principles of free discussion, if any have aught to object to the statement of the committee, we shall feel bound to give a respectful communication a place in our columns; for free discussion is the life of republicanism, and to speak of democracy where free discussion is suppressed would be an abuse of terms.[3]

Thus having acquitted himself of any bias, the editor ran a lengthy statement from the Anti-Slavery Society: "For one man to claim a right of property in another, born equally free, and from the day of his birth to the day of his death hold him as a slave, subject to his absolute will, without any forfeiture of liberty by crime—is a palpable violation of the law of nature and of nature's God." The letter continues by emphasizing that "the whole system is fraught with moral and political evil." It states that slavery "robs God" as well as his children because slaves cannot worship Him whenever, wherever, or however they wish and that it makes a mockery of marriage since God is the one who joins two people together, and with slavery many couples are torn apart. The letter further asserts that this practice "introduces an extensive system of concubinage [*sic*]."

The letter goes on to say that it is not enough to simply pray that God will "avert impending and deserved judgments." "We must *do* something." This call to action included petitioning legislatures to abolish the slave system, circulating antislavery pamphlets, raising funds, and agitating the subject in general. The authors acknowledged that their position was not a popular one, but they were willing to take the high road. "We are called blinded enthusiasts, fanatics, incendiaries, and the like, but we wish not to render railing for railing. We have no unfriendly feelings towards our southern neighbors, but upon christian principles to warn them of their sin and danger before it be too late. . . ."

Having tested the waters with his original column, and receiving no cries of outrage, the editor reported in the next issue that he actually had attended a meeting of the Anti-Slavery Society, something that might be thought foolhardy considering the large pro-slavery element in the county. The meeting, held at Eden, featured three speakers. "[T]here was a remarkable oneness in sentiment," hardly remarkable since the audience consisted of those opposed to slavery. "All concurred in the idea that involuntary slavery was wrong, and that for every wrong there should be a remedy—that the only certain and safe remedy was a general and immediate emancipation . . . that instead of flooding the free States with a colored population, they would be drawn to the south, where they could associate on terms of equality with their own color, find necessary employment, and enjoy the privileges of freemen to a greater extent. . . ."[4]

Even abolitionists, who professed to abhor slavery and love the slave, were not above suggesting solutions that would get the problem away from their doorsteps, such as the proposed resolution to send the local slaves down South. Rationalization and self-justification were the basis of such recommendations. The Covenanter Church in Eden went even further. They supported efforts to send slaves back to their native Africa.

Bethel, Illinois Nov. 20, 1829

Dear Friend,
. . . a contribution was lifted a few days since from the children at [church] $15 in aid for the American Colonization Society. . . .
   I remain yours affectionately

Oliver Bannister

The American Colonization Society, to which Bannister refers, was an early nineteenth-century effort to solve the slave problem. The society had two objectives. First on their agenda was to relocate all African Americans to Liberia in Africa because that was their original homeland. The other objective, perhaps the most influential, was "to get rid of the free Negro in the United States so as to make color caste the permanent foundation of American Negro slavery." Even the Great Emancipator, Abraham Lincoln, was an early proponent of colonization. In a debate with Stephen A. Douglas at Peoria he said, "If all earthly power were given me, I should not know what to do as to the existing institution. My first impulse would be to free all the slaves and send them to Liberia—to their own native land." However, upon reflection, he added that he didn't believe the plan would work.[5]

Lincoln was correct in his assessment of the American Colonization Society. Between 1817 and 1842, the society managed to send approximately 4,000 African Americans to their native continent, but this amounted to an average of 168 per year, less than the average increase in slaves in the United States. Ten times that number "colonized themselves" in Canada for much less than the $386,340 the society spent to relocate others to Africa.[6]

Nationally, Covenanters had endorsed colonization in 1828, with the stipulation that no slaves were to be sent to Africa without their consent. By 1836 the question of resettling Blacks was reconsidered by the church. At that time the church adopted a resolution saying that even though the church has "always considered slavery to be an atrocious sin . . . as much more wicked than common robbery, . . . neither can the sin of slavery justify the sin of banishing the sufferers; nor can we conceive of any thing more injudicious than to transport the heathen of our land to evangelize them on the African shore."[7]

The local Sparta paper indicates that the idea of sending Blacks back to Africa remained alive in Sparta in the years before the Civil War, though it is unlikely, given the reconsidered stance of the Covenanter Church, that the Covenanter congregation in Eden still endorsed the proposition. "All those in favor of the formation of a Colonization Society are requested to meet at the Seminary in Sparta at 2 o'clock on Saturday the 11th of December next."[8]

Sukey couldn't wait while white men formed societies, wrote letters to the newspapers, and held meetings to discuss the blight of slavery on society. She, like so many slaves, took matters into her own hands rather than let others decide her fate. When conditions became horrific for her, she took her sons, and with the help of the girl Hannah, she ran to the home of a known sympathizer, William Hayes, a dairy farmer and devout Covenanter, who lived about eight miles east of the Borders farm.

No evidence has been found that explains how they reached William Hayes. If they traveled by foot and received no rides from sympathetic neighbors, the trip would have taken most of the night.

One route they could have taken is through the creek that lay near their home. It would have provided the safety and security they needed to escape prying eyes. Except in years of unusual rainfall, it rarely has more than a few inches of water. Its bed is clogged with undergrowth and stunted trees, but it is passable, even today, for the foot traveler. After traveling the creek for a few hundred yards, they could have turned north and set off through the countryside, at some point moving eastward toward the sunrise.

How they knew of William Hayes is also a mystery. But in him they found a sympathetic ear to their plight and a man unafraid to defy existing law and help them with their escape.

4

A Great Undertaking

You mention that the Women think it a great undertaking. Just say to them if you have Ordinary health and Prosperity that the great Distress is over when fairly Started. . . . Tell Mrs. Hayes she will be kindly received by her Neighbours.

I remain your Well wisher and Friend

—Andrew Miller to William Hayes,
Randolph County, Illinois, February 18, 1833

William Hayes arrived in Randolph County much later than Andrew Borders, and he took a circuitous route from upstate New York to reach southern Illinois. Hayes had nurtured his fantasy of finding new land for several years, probably beginning when his friends, Andrew Miller and Oliver Bannister, began writing enticing letters about their new homes in Illinois. Hayes appears to be a young adventurer eager to kick the dust of home from his shoes, but he was, in fact, a thirty-eight-year-old father of four who should have been burdened by the responsibilities of raising a young family. The reasons why he chose to turn his back on his elderly mother, brothers, sisters, and a host of other relatives and friends remain a mystery. Still, clues can be found in the many letters written to him in the early years of the nineteenth century.

From a modern vantage point, he seems an unlikely emigrant. In 1833, he had been married for thirteen years, fathered seven children, four of whom were still living, and provided a home for Anna's half sisters, Leah and Jane Cownover. His family obligations should have prevented such flights of fancy. But he, like so many men of his era, saw promise of a richer, fuller life in a new part of the country. Not even his family responsibilities would prevent him from living out his dream. In many ways, this life-altering move determined his destiny.

"The women think it a great undertaking," Andrew Miller wrote. Indeed, it *was* a great undertaking. Anna Hayes must have looked at the venture with dismay, knowing the labor involved in moving a family cross-country and aware that most of it would fall on her shoulders. There were so many problems: Jane Ann was a newborn; at three, Isaac would be difficult to handle; Mary Rachel and Margaret were still so small they would be more burden than help. No doubt the safety and security of home seemed a better option to Anna than setting forth for an unknown future on the frontier.

And then there was the problem of Leah and Jane. It wasn't proper to leave two maiden ladies alone, and taking them along on such a great journey would present its own difficulties. Jane would probably welcome the adventure and be a great help to Anna, but Leah suffered so often from illness that such an undertaking might create hardships beyond her endurance. Anna's head must have spun with the problems her husband's dream had created.

The beauty of Galway in Saratoga County, New York, where they lived, equaled that of anyplace in the country, and in many respects, it surpassed that of Illinois. White pine forests that shipbuilders coveted for their long, straight trunks crowded the primitive trails and lanes leading to village and church. The dark purple humps of the Adirondack Mountains could be glimpsed from their windows, and in springtime, pink and white and gold wildflowers lined the back roads. Saratoga County's thick forests smelled of pine, a pure clean smell that would not be duplicated in Illinois.

Anna, no doubt, hated to give up these scenes of her childhood. She had the security of knowing her half brother, Michael Johnston, lived only a few miles away in Albany, and her half sister, Euphemia Alexander, also lived close by. Perhaps even more important to Anna than her living relatives were the graves in Saratoga County that belonged to her parents and to three of her babies.

Other factors, too, may have played a part in Anna's reluctance to move West. At the time, Illinois was considered to be very unhealthy.

Virtually all settlers suffered from malaria (known as the "ague"), a lack of hygiene, poor diets, and a shortage of trained doctors.[1] The family had already lost children in the "civilized" East; why tempt fate by moving to an area of the country where disease often took babies and old folks, sometimes without warning?

Anna Hayes knew firsthand the pain that came when family members uprooted their lives and moved on. Her own family had been disrupted earlier when her older half sister, Ursulla Taylor, moved with her husband Charles to the Cleveland area of Ohio sometime before 1821. That's when Ursulla's distressing letters began to arrive.

Cleveland June the 16 day 1821

Dear Sister
I Received your leter dated May the 3 in 17 days. I was much pleased to git a letter from you. I had all most give up the ideah of ever Receiving a line from you or Euphemia. My Dear Sisters, you must not forgit me. . . .

Ursulla M. Taylor

"You must not forgit me." Ursulla's plaintive cries of loneliness were easy to discern from the numerous letters she wrote from her new home in Ohio. On the one hand, she says farming there was better than in New York. They were able to plant a greater variety of crops, raised chickens for food, and grew a large assortment of flowers. Such good news, however, was always tempered by the bad.

Cleaveland Ohio July the 25 1821

Dear Mother
. . . I can tell you that Mr. Taylor [her husband] has loast all that he broat in to Ohio, every thing. If he had never got any thing in Schenectady but one of what we had, we now would be rich. Every man that he trusted has broak—sum 2 hundred and 4 hundred dollars. . . .

Ursulla Taylor

In every letter she included comments about her loneliness. On occasion, she turned testy.

Cleaveland Ohio September the 25 1831

Dear Brother and Sisters

I hav not had a letter from you for all most 2 years. I think it straing [strange] indeed. . . . What can be the reason Brother? Am I so worthless that you can't bare to writ me or are you so bissy that you can't take time. So Dear frends if you knowd how much I want to hear from you all Seems to me Som of you Wold hav mersey on me. I love you all. You are with your frends. I am a lone. . . . I am sorry Brother that you do not get reddy to moov in this Country. I like this place much better than when I Saw you. This place has bin quit helthy this year. . . . Dear Sisters if you are in the land of the living pleas to let it be knone by writing to me. . . .

Ursulla Taylor

Surely her sister's loneliness and self-pity caused Anna Hayes to carefully consider if she wanted to put herself and her family in a similar position. Any troubles she had undoubtedly would be easier to tolerate where a strong support system existed.

William, however, had other ideas. Like so many others, he believed that success and riches lay west of the eastern seaboard. Letters from friends like Oliver Bannister and Andrew Miller, who already had moved West, extolled the many fine qualities of the "Illinois Country" and surely influenced his decision to move.

Randolph County, August 6 1830

Dear Friend,

. . . I get more pleased with this Country. . . . If you come you will say it is the best land you have set your eyes on & if you do not come my telling you a fine story would be of little account. . . . I am fully of the opinion that we do & shall have all the happiness here that is possible to be had in this world. . . .

Oliver Bannister

Bannister's wife wrote that she had overcome her initial reluctance to move so far away from home. Her note to Anna, enclosed in her husband's letter, spoke words of comfort.

> Dear Madam
> . . . I think that the [Illinois] contry is helthy, I was disapointed with the plase [at first and] I thought I should not like it I am much pleas with the plase [now] and the people to. I think you would like it if you move to come. your contry is no comparison to this. all this wants is improving. it is knot only good but butifull I see knew beauties arising every day. . . . I wich you and yourse ware hear. I think you never would be sory that you made the exchange. I was like to dispare of the thoughts of starting [but] I sufered more in thoughts than in reality. . . .
>
> I remain your afectnet friend
>
> Eliza Bannister

It is easy to imagine William's excitement as he and his friend, Jonathan Edgcomb, discussed the pros and cons of a scouting trip to Illinois. Their excitement when considering a move West was not unusual in men of that era. Nineteenth-century men constantly looked to better their situation, and most of them thought that no better way existed to improve one's lot in life than to move into the sparsely settled areas west of the Alleghenies. Land of their own, land that had not grown tired from years of overplanting, land where stones never blocked their plow—that's what they hungered for. Best of all, the land they so coveted was economical. Oliver Bannister wrote to tell of the bargains to be had in Illinois.

> Bethel Illinois Nov. 20 A.D. 1829
>
> . . . I am pleased you mention land as low as $15 [in New York] but here is Land for $1.25 which is far superior in point of situation, in the quantity of [illegible], [and] in health of Climate. . . .
>
> I remain yours affectionately
>
> Oliver Bannister

Probably any move seemed attractive to William, since he owned only a portion of the land he farmed. Most of it was owned by his brother-in-law, Michael Johnston, who had inherited it from his and Anna's parents. Since the Hayes family farm had been left to a brother when his father died in 1823, William was left with comparatively little land of his own. Sweating over the green and brown patchwork fields, where every turn of the plow brought up rocks and stones, was doubly difficult when the land didn't belong to him. Then too, Michael wrote a threatening letter indicating he wasn't happy with all that William did.

> Albany July 2, 1827
>
> I wish that you would not cut any more timber off of the land of which you own only the undived [undivided] half as it is injuring the land verry materially depriving me of that which belongs to me of right. and perhaps will if persisted in be the ground of a great deal of unpleasant feeling and unnessary trouble which on other conditions would be avoided. . . .
>
> Michael Johnston

Others, too, were unhappy with William's behavior in regard to property. In a May 9, 1829, letter, an S. L. Vedder and George Shearer threatened him with a lawsuit if he did not stop "taking & carrying off certain property to which we believe you have neither moral nor legal right." Vedder and Shearer asked William to provide a satisfactory explanation for his actions or, they threatened, they would call on him "in a manner less friendly than this is intended to be."

Another letter indicates that William had some financial difficulties in the years prior to 1830, and this may have contributed to his desire to leave New York and find a more hospitable place to live.

April 28, 1829

Dear Sir

Your note (for wheat) has been due a long time. I hope you will see it paid soon without fail.

Yours

Robert Speis
An Executor of John McDermid, deceased

Reading the letters today gives the impression that problems, financial and otherwise, were pressing in on William. Possibly he viewed a move to the western regions of the country as an escape from his predicaments.

Whatever the reasons for William's urge to leave New York, the decision to move away from Saratoga County ultimately became less a question of "if" than of "where." Though Anna objected to any move, she, like most nineteenth-century women, had little control over her husband's decisions. Her duty as a wife lay in following William whenever and wherever he decided to go. Letters indicate he considered three places: Ohio, Randolph County in southern Illinois, and the Military Tract in the central part of Illinois near Peoria. Each had attractions to lure prospective settlers.

Since her half sister, Ursulla Taylor, lived in Ohio, Anna might have preferred that location, but no record of her preference is given in any letter. William seriously considered moving to Ohio because he wrote letters of inquiry about the land available there. His brother-in-law, Charles Taylor, wrote back on January 23, 1830, advising him about the opportunities in Ohio but refused to make any recommendations: "I think you had better view the soil and Situation before you perchis aney ware," he advised.

Enclosed within this letter is a short report from the postmaster at Bucyrus, Ohio, giving details about the land south of Bucyrus. He too cautioned William to visit prospective sites rather than take the "say-so of any man."

[T]he Lands sarruth [south] of Bucyrus (as you have divided them in your letter South & North) are worth Two Dollars per

Acre. They are generally of an excelent quality but nearly destitute of Timber [and have] no Running water although this is easily remydied by diging in which water of a good quality is obtained at a short distance. Those north are Wood Land of a good quality & in my opinion is worth Two Dollars & fifty cents per acre. Very level Laying but not very well watered. Timber principally Beach, Sugar whites, & Black Walnut whites wood ash and some oak. This county is settling very fast and had it not of been there is such a quantity of Government Land unsold and which can be had at one Dollar & Twenty five cents per acre I Should have coted [quoted] this land much higher, but were I the person that was to purchase I should certainly examin it my Selfe without taking the say so of any man.

Yours with respect etc.

[Illegible] John

Oliver Bannister and Andrew Miller, both friends from New York who had settled on the Flat Prairie in Randolph County, Illinois, sent much more detailed descriptions of the land and their lives in that place. The land was home not only to these two friends and their families, but also to a thriving congregation of Covenanter Presbyterians, the church to which William and Anna belonged. Considering the number of letters written that concern church affairs, it is safe to say that the church was a major consideration in any move they made.

However, Randolph County had more to offer than nearby friends and the spiritual sustenance of the church.

Randolph County, Illinois Aug. 13th 1829

Dear Friend

. . . I think the County fully meets my expectation . . . the Children go to school [and] Crab apples and plumbs and grapes are the natural production . . . [also] melons, peaches. . . . I hope you will come to see this Country. I am sure you will like it & more especially the people. tell Mrs. Hayes that the big hog is Dead & I haven't [seen] but one or two snakes in the State. . . . There is no water mill here but . . . a steam mill is going up . . . a saw mill is greatly needed here. . . . Here is a great congregation attentive [and] desirous to assist. . . .

Oliver Bannister

Family folklore passed down through the generations says that Anna Hayes had a dreadful fear of snakes, so Bannister's mention of them may have been another attempt to allay her fears about moving.

The region where Bannister and Miller lived lay a mile or so from the small village of Eden. At the time Hayes left New York, Eden consisted of "two spacious churches and a few dwellings around them." Settlers had great hopes for the little settlement, and most expected it to grow into an important town. By 1837 it had a population of three hundred people, a dry goods store, four wagon shops, one carriage and plow manufactory, one school, a literary society, a large library, a saddlery shop, and a few other businesses.[2]

The town of Columbus lay two miles to the west. Though it wasn't settled until a few years after Eden, it soon became a formidable rival. More and more settlers began moving there, and by 1839, when it changed its name to Sparta, it had become the center of population in the northeastern section of Randolph County. Through the years, Eden failed to live up to its potential, and eventually it lost every business and most of its population. Today Eden is what is euphemistically known as "a wide place in the road." In contrast, Sparta's population soon numbered into the thousands, and the town had not only churches and wagon shops but also doctors, schools, a newspaper, and a host of flourishing retail businesses.[3]

The third option William considered lay in the Military Tract in central Illinois. This cornucopia-shaped tract of land encompassed all the ground between the Mississippi and Illinois rivers and extended north to the Rock River. This section of the state was called the Military Tract because the government "patented" it in quarter sections (160 acres) and gave it to veterans of the War of 1812 in payment for their military service. Though a few actually moved to the Illinois country, veterans rarely considered the land of much value or thought to live on it themselves. Squatters eventually inhabited much of the land and made rudimentary "improvements" (in some cases little more than a hastily constructed shack) that increased its worth. When William considered moving, he looked at land near the present-day city of Peoria on the Illinois River.

It is likely that William Hayes had access to property in the Military Tract before he left to examine the options available. Anna's cousin, Robert Johnston, wrote:

New York 2nd October 1832

Mr. Wm Hay[e]s
. . . I have just paid the taxes on that lot in Illinoise . . . they have been raise fifty four cent I have paid six 50/100 dollars it has not been sold for taxes. the whole expence I have been at has been seven 50/100 Dollars. . . . I have not gote in posession. the man that I promised to sell it to has got it and I have not been able to get it. I shall get it soon. . . .

Robt. R. Johnston

Robert Johnston's letter seems to indicate that someone in the family, perhaps Johnston himself, was a veteran of the 1812 war and would sell or perhaps give his patent to William Hayes. Further evidence of this link to the Military Tract is found in letters from Oliver Bannister and Andrew Miller.

Randolph Ill, Feb. 18th A.D. 1833

Dear Friend
We are mutch pleased to learn from your letter that you are all well & the more so that you intend to visit our Country. . . . I think it best for your family to come forward with you. . . . I must insist a little on this as I want to see Mrs. Hayes. Your Military Land is of little value here. . . .

Oliver Bannister

Feb. 1833

Dear Friend
. . . I am hapy to learn that you have at length concluded to
Visit this land of pleanty, . . . Your Military land I think will do
little good. I have no Doubt but it may be of a good quality but
the Taxes will soon eat it up. . . . I know you have a Strong
Desire to see the Western Sexions in all their Diversities.
Perhaps when you come here you will think with myself all
things considered we are about as well off as any of our
neighbours. . . .
    I remain your Well wisher and Friend

Andrew Miller

In many ways, William Hayes was typical of the pioneers who traveled westward in the nineteenth century. Like most of those who uprooted their families, he yearned for a better, more prosperous life for
his family—something he probably felt could be more easily obtained
if he owned rich, new land in an area that was wide open to settlers. By
the 1830s, when he was seriously considering relocating, "modern"
methods of travel made the trip west far easier than it had ever been.
The Erie Canal opened in 1825 to provide economical, fast transit for
passengers. Steamboats began plying the Great Lakes in 1830, and
though they were dangerous at times, most people eagerly used them
to cut journey time to a minimum.

However, Hayes was an atypical pioneer; evidence suggests that he
carefully and thoroughly researched his options. Many emigrants, especially those from the South, simply packed their few belongings and
started out not knowing exactly where they would land. If one place
didn't suit, well, there were other places somewhere ahead that might
be better. Northerners like William Hayes were more thorough in
their research and narrowed their choices before starting out.

By the winter of 1833, William Hayes had decided to move. The
trip he planned would not be merely a visit to relatives in Cleveland or
friends in Illinois. Though he had not yet decided where the family
would eventually settle, the plans he made suggest that he would not

return to live in upstate New York. This trip would be a permanent relocation.

William and Anna took their four children, Anna's two half sisters, and a friend, Jonathan Edgecomb, on their trip to the West. Their plan, however, did not include taking the women and children the entire way—at least not at first. They were to stay in Cleveland with Charles and Ursulla Taylor until William and Jonathan returned from a scouting foray into Illinois. No doubt one reason they were to remain in Cleveland was to give Anna and her sisters a chance for a long visit with Ursulla, whom they had not seen since 1826. From a more practical standpoint, it would be easier to scout the land if the men weren't hampered by having to provide for women and children.

William and Anna's family remaining in New York were not pleased with his intention to relocate so far from home. Of special concern to Michael Johnston was the plight of Leah and Jane Cownover. Though he was only their stepbrother, he obviously felt close enough to them to worry about their well-being. He thought it especially foolhardy for Leah to accompany the Hayes family on a long and difficult journey to the West. He wrote in a letter addressed to Leah:

Albany April 12th 1833

Dear Sister

We understand by William Hayes that you intend moving with him to the west. We think the undertaking is too great for you in your tender and delicate state of health & therefore We shall offer you a few reasons why He should advise you not to go. . . .

First and foremost among his reasons were Leah's "delicate state of health," which he described as "sudden attacks" that would make such an arduous journey both "tedious and irksome if not dangerous." The second reason he cited was her age, though she was only fifty-two at the time. At such an advanced age, he warned, it would be difficult and "unpleasant" to form new friends. The fact that she was going with family was not a good reason to jeopardize the friendships she had acquired over a lifetime.

Thirdly, Michael felt that leaving upstate New York would be detrimental to Leah's spiritual health because she was going to a place not populated with pastors and congregations that shared their strict Covenanter Presbyterian upbringing. He warned that it would be dangerous to associate with people "who have forsaken the truth."

His final appeal was an emotional one. "You have friends here that wish you to stay." If, as he suspected, she was moving just because she would be homeless when the Hayes family left, he wanted to assure her that she would always have a home with people who knew her, though he stops short of inviting her to share his home.

> If you should desire to come to Albany . . . we do assure
> you that you have here [people] who would willingly while it
> is in their power to take delight in accomodating you with a
> home. . . .
>   Please to show these lines to your sister Jane for her consider-
> ation as we intend them for her too. . . . Farewell & fare you
> well.
>   Your brother
>
> Michael Johnston

Though Michael had included the invitation to Jane, as well as Leah, he seems to have fewer concerns about Jane, perhaps because, at forty-two, she was ten years younger than Leah and seems to have been in good health.

Michael's reasons failed to convince Leah to stay in New York. Both she and Jane elected to accompany William and Anna to Illinois. Both remained throughout their lifetimes, and both are buried in the Hayes family plot in Caledonia Cemetery in Sparta.

Though the exact date of departure is unknown, the entire Hayes household, including William's friend, Jonathan Edgcomb, left Galway in late May or early June of 1833. Had Anna known what lay ahead, she might have resisted the move much more forcefully.

5

The "Jurney"

Should you think of coming straight on to this place with the famely make your agreement to leave the Steemboat on the Mississippi at Chester below the Mouth of [the] Okaw [now called the Kaskaskia River] ever inquire for Flat Prairie—There is a location made for a carriage at the Town Columbus [now Sparta] about one and a half miles from our Church. . . . Wishing all Prosperity to you and famely with Success in your Jurney I remain your Well wisher and Friend

—Andrew Miller to William Hayes,
Randolph County, Illinois, February 18, 1833

Though Andrew Miller hoped William and his family would come straight to Randolph County, that was not to be the case. Besides having access to property in the Military Tract, Hayes seems to have been the type who made plans and stuck to them.

The exact route the party took to reach Illinois is unknown, but they probably boarded a boat on the Erie Canal to travel to Buffalo, New York. There, they would have caught a steamboat on Lake Erie for the comparatively short trip to the Cleveland area, where Anna's half sister Ursulla Taylor lived, following much the same route that Oliver Bannister described in an 1829 letter.

Randolph County Illinois Aug. 13th 1829

Dear Friend
After I left you I hired a Boat at Schenectady for $25, which landed us all safely at Buffalo on the following Monday

morning in good health. here we lay two days. the storm was
so great that none dare go out—the drought has been so great
that we cannot get down the Allegany. . . . July 1st on board
the steam Boat Enterprise bound to Detroit we had a terrible
storm & I found Lake Erie to be what I heard it was. We were all
sea-sick—but landed safely at Sandusky City (a mean place for
travellers) on the morning of the 2nd. we should have suffered
were it not for the kindness of a widow who filled our hearts
with joy. this 200 miles cost us 17 Dollars. . . .

    In the Lord

             Oliver Bannister

Letters written by family members indicate that those left behind in
New York were troubled about William and Anna. Using the primitive postal service meant that time dragged between letters. As days,
then weeks, then months passed without hearing from them,
William's family imagined all sorts of calamities. Indeed, sickness had
plagued the Hayes family, and William had suffered an unspecified accident on a steamboat—probably the one they used to cross Lake Erie.

                Galway October 15, 1833

Dear Brother and Sister Leah and Jaine and to the
Dear Children
I hardly no how to begin to write to you fore my hart is so full at
the thought of our beaing so far Seperated from each other. . . . I
have had much uneasiness about you sins your last letter . . . as
you was thene Sick. . . . last weak we herd that you was all well
by Mr. Edgcombs Letter that he Sent home. I think you have
had many trials sines you left us and hardships such as you never
experienced before but I feal as thow God had bene on your
right hand for good in Spareing youre lives threw so many
Daingers. . . .

    My love to you all

           Polly Jones [William's sister]

Galway, October 29, 1833

Dear Brother

. . . Received a letter from you about the 20 of September and
we ware verry sorry to hear that you met with a misfortune
yourself on the Steamboat and that Ann and the little Boy ware
Sick with the fever ague. We are looking for Mr. Edgcomb home
soon and we are verry anxious to sea him as we understand that
he has been at your place. . . . Tell Ann that she must wright. . .
. we expect that she has sean a great deal of troubl since she left
Galway. You must wright how little Jane Ann does now as you
wrought that she was unwell. . . .

Isaac Hayes [William's brother]

Anna, Leah, Jane, and the children stayed to visit with the Taylors
in Ohio for about a month. After inspecting acreage in Ohio, William
and Jonathan set out for the Military Tract in Illinois. Once there, they
intended to examine the land to see if the place would be suitable.
Apparently, no decision would be made until they had inspected land
in Illinois. William's brother, Isaac, had definite ideas about where
William should settle.

Galway June the 28 1833

Dear Brother

. . . [Y]ou [Anna] wrought that William had started for
the Illanois and that he Expected to be gone about four
Weeks when he Returns I want he should wright a long
letter and to wright how he is Pleased with that Country
and whether you Expect to settle in the Illinois. I think if
you like the State of Ohio you had better Settle there for I
think that then you are far enough away from you[r]
Friends but if you should think of Mooveing to the State of
illenois I want you to wright and to wright whether you
will be down to Galway before you should go. . . .

We remain your friends and wellwishers

Isaac and Jane Hayes

The Illinois River meandered slowly through a valley two to five miles wide when William and Jonathan visited the Military Tract in 1833. The river had been discovered by Sieur Louis Jolliet, a French Canadian, and Father Jacques Marquette, a French Jesuit priest, more than 150 years before William arrived, but little had changed since Jolliet and Marquette first saw the stream they called the "St. Louis." In his diary, dated 1673, Fr. Marquette wrote:

> We have seen nothing like this river that we enter, as regards its fertility of soil, its prairies and woods, its cattle, elk, deer, wild cats, bustards [wild game birds], swans, ducks, parroquets, and even beaver. . . . The river which we have named the St. Louis and which rises near the lower end of the Lake of Illinois seemed to me to be the most beautiful and the most suitable for settlement. . . . This river is wide and deep, filled with catfish and sturgeons. Game is there in abundance, oxen cows, stags, does, Turkeys, in much greater numbers than elsewhere. . . . There are prairies of six, ten and 20 leagues in length and three wide, surrounded by forests of the same extent.[1]

When William and Jonathan came to the Illinois River valley, the little town of Peoria consisted of seven frame homes and approximately twenty-one primitive log cabins, but it was the largest settlement on that part of the frontier. Peoria County, in which it was located, had scarcely fifteen hundred citizens.[2]

Peoria's location was beautiful beyond description. Situated on a high limestone bluff overlooking the Illinois River, the town was known as an important point for trading. Its location was auspicious because communication by steamboat and stage kept the village in touch with neighboring settlements. By 1834 Peoria's population was between three hundred and four hundred; a year later, it had doubled in size.

Peoria had first been known as "Fort Clark," a fort constructed by Americans during the War of 1812 and named for General George Rogers Clark. Standing at the foot of what are now Liberty and Water Streets, the fort was used only a few years, then fell into disrepair. In

1818 it was burned by Indians. Though the town name changed in 1825 to Peoria, after the Peoria Indian tribe, William Hayes received mail addressed to "Fort Clark" as late as 1834.

The prairies bordering the Illinois River were sparsely settled in 1833. To anyone used to the sprawl and activity of eastern cities, it may have seemed desolate and lonely. More than one family had pulled up stakes and moved on. William Hayes came to the Military Tract at the peak of its development, when most pioneers chose to settle along the riverbanks. The prairie land seemed unproductive to early nineteenth-century farmers because prevailing thought of the day held that if land could not grow trees, it certainly wouldn't grow crops. Once the land along the rivers had been settled, though, more and more pioneers ventured out on the prairie to break the tough sod and plant their seed. Experience soon taught them that the rich prairie land produced harvests more bountiful than the woodlands ever could.

In 1833 the Illinois River ran clear and clean below the limestone bluffs on which Peoria was located, just as it had when Jolliet and Marquette discovered it. The water teemed with fish of astonishing size; lacy green leaves still shadowed the forests bordering the water; and limitless prairies still stretched for miles, hampered only occasionally by clumps of ancient oak trees. In the summer, tall grasses and slender reeds sprinkled with purple and gold and pink wildflowers stood high as a person's head on the prairies. One early traveler described the prairies as a "fairy-like scene on which the eye delights to dwell."[3]

In autumn the land was barren, often blackened and laid waste by fire. In winter snow covered the vast, trackless prairies, and bitter winds howled without ceasing. Spring brought rain in such amounts that trails often turned into soggy sloughs that mired men and beasts alike.

Many guidebooks to the Illinois country were available at the time, and it is likely that William Hayes consulted one or more of them before leaving New York. He would have been fairly well educated about what to expect when he arrived in Illinois.[4]

William and Jonathan, no doubt, scrutinized the region with a farmer's eye, looking at the fertility of the soil, the proximity of accessible water, the availability of woodlands from which to build a house or cabin, and details about regional weather. Personal safety, of course, was also a concern.

Indians had caused problems just the year before, when Black Hawk, a Sauk chief, led a group of his followers from their winter hunting ground in Iowa west of the Mississippi to begin spring planting at their ancestral home near Prophetstown, as they usually did. The Federal government had been "persuading" the Indians to move west of the Mississippi for several years, and Black Hawk's defiance of government orders panicked the white settlers. Governor John Reynolds responded by calling out the militia—a call that was heard and answered by young men all across the state, including one scrawny twenty-three-year-old Sangamon County resident named Abraham Lincoln.

Black Hawk sent appeals to other Indian tribes to help him, but few responded. Consequently, the Indians were soundly whipped at the battle of Bad Axe, and Black Hawk himself was captured by members of the Winnebago tribe and turned over to the United States government. By the time William and his family arrived on the Illinois River, settlers hoped the Indian "problem" had been solved once and for all in the Illinois country.

Despite some drawbacks, Illinois had many things in its favor to draw settlers to its boundaries. From 1831 to 1840, the postal routes in Illinois were increased from 3,276 miles to 6,690 miles, land offices increased from six to ten, and all Indian titles to land had been revoked. This nine-year period saw a huge increase in land sales. In 1831 only 1,838,601 acres of land had been sold in Illinois; by 1840, 9,120,947 acres had been sold to incoming settlers. The population jumped during this period from 155,000 to over half a million people.[5]

William Hayes apparently liked what he saw on the banks of the Illinois River, for there are no indications that he traveled to southern Illinois at this time. He either purchased or claimed acreage in the Military Tract and sent for or traveled back to Ohio to get the rest of the family. Jonathan Edgcomb, however, decided to return to New York State, a journey that took more than a month.

In November Jonathan wrote telling about his trip. His letter gives information about how arduous travel could be in the mid-nineteenth century. By September 25 he decided he had seen enough and made plans to head back to New York. Though he had not yet decided to settle near William, he couldn't resist giving his opinion about the new courthouse being built in Peoria. He was interested in it, he said, because "I may come there yet."

Sch'dy, NY

Nov. 23, 1833

Respected friend

. . . I hope your court house Commissioner will not put your court house in the Middle of the Square. It will Spoil the Look of the place to put a Court house in the Square with a high Steeple, tell them to Send to Cleveland Ohio or to Elyria, Lorrain Co. just west of Cleveland. Either is well Laid out at the Square and the Court houses are fine moddles. I feel an Interest in this Matter for I may come there yet. There should be no Steeple to a Courthouse, but a Cupalo or Dome on the top. . . .

Affectionate yours,

Jonathan Edgcomb

Little is known about William and Anna's life in Peoria. Letters from family members indicate William was well pleased with his new life on the banks of the Illinois River. In a February 14, 1834, letter, Hayes's brother-in-law, Thomas Alexander, states that "we all Rejoiced to here that you and family ware all in comfortable circumstances."

Several other correspondents refer to letters William had written urging his brothers and sisters to come to Illinois to visit them in their new home. No one, however, was willing or able to do so.

Anna Hayes may not have been as pleased as William with their new life in Illinois. Certainly Ursulla Taylor implies that at least some of the family in Illinois were unhappy with the situation. She blamed William for taking her sisters so far away.

Cleaveland Ohio June 1834

Dear Brother and Sisters all 3

... I am afraid that sum of you will Stay and greav yourselves to
deth I do hope you will Sel and Com back. I can't think that
William don right in going so far. It seemes as if he was
determand to bee away from all frends and relatives and good
preaching. ...

Farewell

Ursulla M. Taylor

Other letters tell why Anna was dissatisfied with their new home. It
appears that she and Leah had contracted malaria, though letters written from New York seem ignorant of the symptoms.

Galway May 7th 1834

Dear Brother and Sister

... [Y]ou mentioned that sister Ann and leah still kep a trem-
bling and shaking with the cold I think it curious to that they
can't keep from being Cold in the summer time and in so warm
a country to I think you have not much wood in that country or
you could [keep] from freezing yourself and keep them warm to.
...

Yours affectionly

John Alexander 2nd

[William's brother-in-law]

Malaria, called the "ague" by early settlers, was an ever-present
threat in the marshy land around Peoria. In 1821 Henry Schoolcraft,
an early explorer and ethnologist, visited the area and saw numerous
women shaking with malaria, many of them so ill they could not care
for their children. This scourge of the prairies was responsible for a
great deal of suffering and death, and for a time it slowed down settlement in the Illinois River valley.

Despite Anna's illness, William began dabbling in real estate. Land
speculation in Illinois had reached an all-time high, and ambitious
men bought and sold land as a means of increasing the family income.

During his travels over the countryside, he probably made many contacts and became familiar with the land in central Illinois—all information that would serve him well when he became immersed in illicit activities involving escaping slaves.

No matter how successful he became in his new ventures, though, he could not ignore the decline in Anna's health. After spending less than a year in central Illinois, he decided to move again.

Galena Sept 18th 1834

> Dear friends,
> . . . Sir on the acount of your wifs want of health I was
> happey to here that you had sold your land. I am happey that
> you made out well . . . and I hope where you are going you will
> not be so mutch troubled with the ague as you have been about
> peoria. . . .
> your wellwisher
>
> John Shedden

Records indicate that William Hayes purchased 160 acres of land in the Flat Prairie, located outside Eden, over the space of four years. Each plot of land was purchased in 40-acre increments and cost a total of $254.69.[6]

6

Next Neighbours

[The] hens [prairie chickens] here have a good living.
they are the same size of common fowls & do very well
to cook. they are very plenty. I suppose 150 held a
meeting every morning near my door untill they concluded their number grew smaller because so many fell
into our pot.

—Oliver Bannister to William Hayes,
Bethel, Randolph County, Illinois, January 1830

Bannister's humor and enthusiasm for his new home in Randolph County bubbles from the pages of his letters to William. Besides the numerous prairie chickens that fell into his pot, he could see four houses from his doorstep, a sign, at least to him, that the county was growing and prospering at a great rate. He puzzled over the fact that Andrew Miller had such abundant crops: "[W]hen Mr. Miller began his farm the Inhabitants were surprised he should take such a poor lot" (apparently, Miller had chosen prairie land over woodland).

In addition to superior crops, Bannister was proud that he had the only oven within "18 miles either way." Added to this was his prediction that the county "will be a great wool country" except for a large wolf population that needed to be killed.

Bannister's excitement about Randolph County surely influenced William, for when Anna became sick and longed to leave Peoria, he immediately moved his family to southern Illinois. No evidence exists that he ever considered moving back to New York. They probably arrived in the fall of 1834 because by December he received mail addressed to "Bethel, Shannon's P. O. Randolph Co., Ill." Andrew

Miller had written earlier that land adjoining his would soon be available.

Illinois Randolph County Bethel 15 June 1832

> Dear Friend
> . . . If you think to come here there is Section of land joining with me Said to be the best in this Township Expected to be Sold by next Spring. it is the School Section and Could not be Sold without leave from the State. it is expected the State will grant leave this Winter. Should this happen you and me might yet live next neighbours. . . .
> I remain your constant friend
>
> Andrew Miller

They did indeed become "next neighbours." William and Anna settled with their family on a farm in Flat Prairie, about two miles east of Columbus and one mile north of Eden, where William intended to continue his vocation as a dairy farmer—an occupation that did not require the fertile fields found in central Illinois.

"Flat Prairie" seems to be redundant terminology, but in regard to the prairies of the region, it is an apt description. Randolph County was largely covered by woodlands in the 1830s. Unlike the vast prairies in the central part of the state, the prairie lands of Randolph County tend to be small and rolling, and sections near Kaskaskia and Prairie du Rocher feature tall, limestone bluffs overlooking the Mississippi River. Flat Prairie, however, is larger than most prairies in the county and is unusual because it is fairly level and, for the most part, devoid of trees. A large, flat expanse of land in this section of Illinois is something special and extraordinary, so the appellation of "Flat Prairie" is not redundant; it is terminology that reflects the unique nature of the land.

The soil in Flat Prairie is composed of a rich, sandy loam. While it is not the dark, fertile soil found in central Illinois, it is adequate for raising a variety of crops. Early farmers primarily raised cotton and corn, and later the castor bean became a prominent crop. Still later, wheat became the chief product.

The move to the southern part of the state did not mean that William intended to give up his land speculating business. At the end of December, A. Hall, probably a business acquaintance, sent William a hundred dollars "in one bill," indicating that William had ongoing business in Peoria County.

Peoria December 31 1834

Dear Sir

... At your request I Send you one hundred Dollars in one bill the reason I have not Sent it Before was that I did not receive the money untill the 27th and then it was in Silver and Small Bills and I did not git exchang Soon enough to go out in the mail I have endorsed one hundred Dollars on the Note you gave which will only leave the interest due. ...

A. Hall

Though the Bannister, Miller, and Hayes families originated in upstate New York, most of the emigrants who settled in the Sparta area came from the southern states. Many of them emigrated because they opposed slavery and could no longer tolerate a society that enslaved other human beings and treated them as a subhuman species. Rather than fight for their beliefs, they chose to move where they hoped slavery would not be a daily problem. Most of them were Scots-Irish in heritage and came from the Abbeville District of North Carolina.

However, another type of Southerner also moved to Randolph County because of its lenient attitude toward slavery. Andrew Borders was representative of this type of Southerner, and he was not alone. In these early years, Randolph County contained 234 slaves, 137 of them in the county seat of Kaskaskia. Only five slaveholders lived near Andrew Borders in the Plum Creek Township, located west of Sparta.[1] Borders was decidedly in the minority in this section of the county and easily was the focus of much antislavery sentiment.

It is likely that William Hayes belonged to the Randolph County Anti-Slavery Society because its meetings were held in his church and letters from family members in New York confirmed that he was engaged in helping "the Blacks with a ride." He, as well as others living near Eden, were *doing* something about the intolerable conditions of slavery—something far more valuable than distributing antislavery tracts and petitioning the state legislature on behalf of the enslaved.

The move to Flat Prairie and Randolph County must have been an excellent choice for the Hayes family, for they never moved again. Anna apparently regained her health, and they were able to obtain acreage near their old friends, Eliza and Oliver Bannister and Peggy and Andrew Miller.

Sometime before 1840 they built a snug, frame house—a house that still stands—on the prairie to shelter their growing family. At last they lived near close friends who could supply them with the sense of family that had been missing in the Military Tract. Perhaps even more importantly, they were able to join the thriving congregation of Covenanter Presbyterians who had established a church on a small rise in the prairie—a place so beautiful that the town that grew around it would be called Eden. Here the Rev. Samuel Wylie could give them the "good preaching" that Ursulla Taylor had wanted for them, and they would be part of a Christian community whose articles of faith would have a profound effect on William Hayes in the years to come.

Andrew and Martha Borders, as depicted in the
Illustrated Historical Atlas of Randolph County, Illinois, 1875.
(Courtesy of the Sparta Public Library)

Belleville, Jan. 1. 1845

Mr. Hays:

Dear Sir:

I returned from Spring-
field a few days ago. Before I left
your case against Borders was argued
in the Supreme court by Baker and
Koerner for Borders, and by Trumbull
and myself in your behalf. We had a
long and desperate struggle but I
am very confident that we will
reverse the judgment below.

On a careful examination I found that
the old Court of Common pleas was
abolished four years before the time
Sukey was registered, and her register
was of course a nullity.

We had also decisions that the indentures of the children were not
binding on them and that they are
void also.

We produced law that in a case
like this, that the master of Sukey
could not recover the price of her
whole term of service before it expired. Field
instructed the jury below the contrary

In haste

Yours respectfully
W. H. Underwood

P.S. I will write you again as soon as
I get the decision of the court.
Bannisters case against Reed & Brown
we also argued before I left.
I hope to hear from or see you
soon.

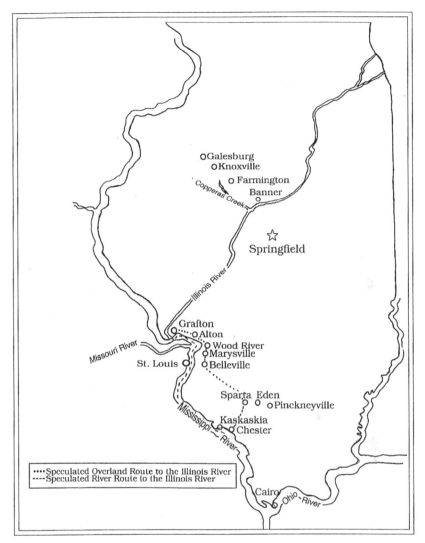

Map showing two possible routes the fugitives and William Hayes may have taken to reach the Illinois River on their way to northern Illinois. (Copyright 1999 by W. Terry Waldron)

(Opposite) Copy of an 1845 letter from attorney William Underwood to his client, William Hayes, describing Underwood's appearance before the Illinois Supreme Court in Springfield. (Courtesy of Mr. and Mrs. James V. Hayes)

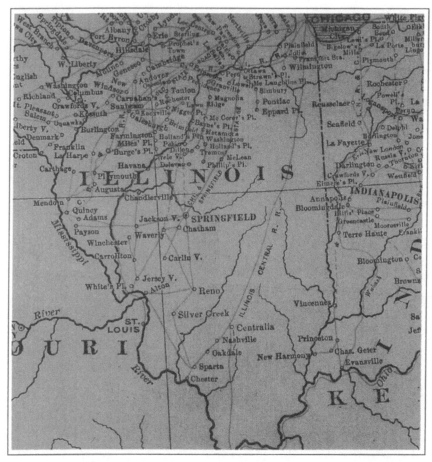

The Illinois portion of Wilbur Henry Siebert's "Underground Routes to Canada," in *The Underground Railroad*, 1898. Many of the routes and stations of the Underground Railroad in Illinois correspond to Covenanter settlements. (Courtesy of the Illinois State Historical Library)

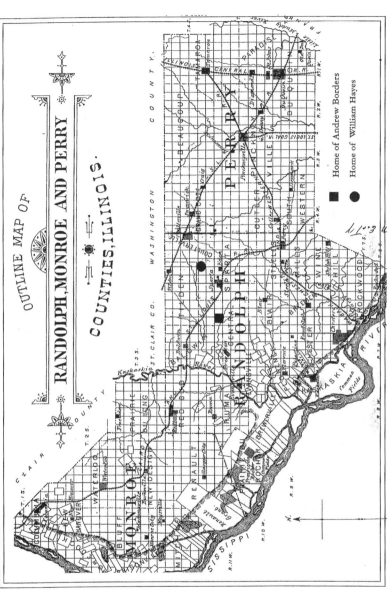

Map of the tri-county area, from the *Combined History of Randolph, Monroe, and Perry Counties, Illinois*, 1883. Shown are the location of the homes of Andrew Borders and William Hayes. (Courtesy of the Sparta Public Library)

Drawing of the Knox County Jail, from the *History of Knox County, Illinois*, 1878. (Courtesy of the C. E. Brehm Memorial Library, Mt. Vernon)

Photo of the Knox County Courthouse. (Courtesy of the Illinois State Historical Library)

Photo of the farm home of William Hayes. Hayes's home, built sometime before 1840, is still owned by his descendants. The two-story addition was built in 1929. (Courtesy of Mr. and Mrs. James V. Hayes)

Photo of William H. Bissell.
Bissell represented Andrew
Borders in the Perry County
trial. (Courtesy of the Illinois
State Historical Library)

Photo of Gustave Koerner.
Koerner also served as
legal counsel for Borders in
Borders v. Hayes.
(Courtesy of the Illinois
State Historical Library)

Photo of Lyman Trumbull.
Trumbull led William
Hayes's defense team at his
trial in 1844. (Courtesy of
the Illinois State Historical
Library)

Photo of James Shields.
Shields presided as judge at
the Perry County trial.
(Courtesy of the Illinois
State Historical Library)

Photo of Jesse B. Thomas. Thomas wrote the majority opinion in the Illinois Supreme Court decision in *Hay{e}s v. Borders*, December 1844. (Courtesy of the Illinois State Historical Library)

Photo of Samuel D. Lockwood. Lockwood authored the minority opinion in *Hay{e}s v. Borders*. (Courtesy of the Illinois State Historical Library)

7

The Covenanters

We have had Mr. Wylie every Sabbath but one—he
comes forth as a bold Champion of the Everlasting
Gospel & preaches to a larger congregation. I am mutch
pleased with his witness & good performance.
> —Oliver Bannister to William Hayes,
> Bethel, Randolph County, Illinois, November 20, 1829

William and Anna Hayes were devoted members of a branch of
Reformed Presbyterianism who called themselves Covenanters. The northeastern section of Randolph County was settled largely
by the Covenanters, and in many ways their beliefs affected William
Hayes when he began his work with escaping slaves.

The numerous letters written to William and Anna referring to
church matters, both in New York and Illinois, testify to the importance of the church in their lives. They frequently kept visiting minis-
ters in their home, and after they moved to Illinois, family members
and friends discussed church doctrine and included church gossip in
their letters to them. Certainly, the church was a major authority in
both their lives, and it undoubtedly influenced William's moral and
ethical values.

Covenanters adhered to a strict interpretation of the Bible and held
several views that were contrary with the beliefs of most other Protestant denominations, even other branches of Presbyterianism. For example, Covenanters held no allegiance to either state or federal governments because their constitutions did not recognize Jesus as head
of the State. In fact, the Covenanter church "looked upon it [the gov-
ernment] as 'an heathen and unbaptized government' which denies

Christ. . . ."[1] Because of this particular belief, Covenanters challenged governmental authority at every opportunity. They refused to work on the roads a few days each year, as was the custom at the time. They did not vote in elections, would not serve on juries or hold any government office, or do anything else that showed recognition of the government. Many of these doctrines persisted in the Covenanter Church well into the twentieth century, particularly their attitude about not exercising their right to vote in national and state elections.

Covenanters voted only once in any election before the 1960s. They voted in 1824 because an election was held to change the Illinois State Constitution. In essence, the outcome of the election would decide whether Illinois would be slave or free. Devout Covenanters wholeheartedly believed that the state should be free of a system that held other people in bondage. At that time, they made their voices heard by means of the ballot when they voted unanimously against slavery.

Despite their efforts, 55 percent of Randolph County residents voted with the pro-slavery faction, making the county one of only a handful that voted to retain a system of indenture within the state.[2] Statewide, the majority of voters were against the legal introduction of slavery into Illinois.

Covenanters had a long history of opposition to the slavery system. Beginning around 1800, they actively supported abolitionism. In 1801 they refused communion to slaveholders—one of the first denominations to do so.[3] Well before the Civil War, they opened their churches to abolitionist speakers, belonged to antislavery societies, and worked in the Underground Railroad.[4] A map drawn by Wilbur Henry Siebert, "the pioneer student of the Underground Railroad," shows that the locations of known Underground Railroad stations in southern Illinois were located in areas of Covenanter settlements.[5]

Bethel Church at Eden may have been more outspoken than most on the subject of slavery. Theodore Pease, in writing his history of Illinois, mentions "the little Reformed Presbyterian group at Sparta and Eden who on occasion went so far as to pronounce the dissolution of a union tainted with slavery as not the worst misfortune that might befall."[6]

Another Covenanter belief concerned the singing of hymns. They believed, and still believe, that only Psalms should be sung in their worship services, and they should not be accompanied by any musical instrument. They believe that the organ and other musical instruments have no place in a worship service because no scriptural evidence exists to support use of man-made instruments. For Covenanters, only the human voice is necessary to praise God.[7] These two particular doctrines set them apart today from all other Protestant denominations.

The Bethel Church in Eden predates all other Protestant churches in Randolph County. In 1817, the year before Illinois became a state and long before William and Anna arrived in Randolph County, a twenty-eight-year-old graduate of the University of Pennsylvania and the Theological Seminary at Philadelphia rode his horse through the southern part of Illinois and into Missouri on a scouting trip to determine an area ripe for missionary work. His name was Samuel Wylie. He had been sent by the Middle Presbytery of the Reformed Presbyterian Church, located in Pennsylvania.

Rev. Wylie, like so many exploring the western lands of the country, was an immigrant. He had been born in County Antrim in Northern Ireland in 1790 and came to Pennsylvania at the age of seventeen. After graduating from college and seminary, he was licensed to preach in 1815. The Middle Presbytery, after hearing his reports of the Illinois country, sent him back to Randolph County in July of 1818. He immediately began his work in the largely Roman Catholic town of Kaskaskia. Soon, however, Covenanters began arriving in the county.

Rev. Wylie purchased the land that is now the town of Eden, perhaps with no thought of founding a community. However, as Covenanter Presbyterians began moving into Randolph County, Rev. Wylie collected together enough to form a church, and the village sprang up around it.

In 1819 the congregation issued a call for Rev. Wylie to be their permanent pastor. This new congregation was called "Bethel," which in Hebrew means "house of God." This congregation eventually provided a spiritual home to the William Hayes family, as well as to his friends, Oliver Bannister and Andrew Miller.

At the time of Wylie's installation in 1821, the Bethel congregation probably consisted of seventy-five to one hundred people, with more Covenanters pouring into the county every day.[8] In the beginning, they met in cabins, barns, and beneath the trees in the forest, but this arrangement didn't suit them for long. In 1823 the congregation built a new church, only twenty-eight by forty feet. This first building soon became inadequate because so many Covenanters flocked to the area. Oliver Bannister reported they were forced out under the trees on special days when the crowds were too numerous to be contained within the building. Plans were made for a new building in 1827, but work didn't get under way until 1830.

August 6, 1830

> Dear Friend
> . . . We are building a Brick Meeting House 60 by 45 ft. Its
> expected twill cost at the outside about $1200, it will make a
> fine show from its elevated situation . . . from Mr. Millers
> Statement who is Chairman of the building Committee twill
> cost as mutch more to finish the inside. Mr. Wylie is a worthy
> man seeking the peace & happiness of his people. . . .
>
> Oliver Bannister

Unfortunately, the "peace and happiness" Mr. Wylie supposedly wanted for his congregation didn't occur because a bitter fight began over the location of the new church. Some wanted it to remain in the lowland near the cemetery where the original building stood, but others, equally vocal, thought it should be on the elevated rise in the prairie where the present-day town of Eden is located. The ensuing controversy caused a split in the congregation.

Illinois Randolph County Bethel

15 June 1832

Dear Friend

. . . Since Mr. Millican [perhaps a mutual friend] left us the
congregation is Divided. About fifty five Members asked and
obtained a disjunction from Mr. Wylie. Mr. Millican would tell
you of the trouble that existed in the Congregation about the
Building a new house. It is rather expected that they will yet
return. . . .

I remain your Constant Friend

Andrew Miller

Miller reported that the "new house" was completed and that the
church had been "decently filled" for a service. He also stated that several new Covenanter congregations had been organized, one "twelve
miles distant where there was not a single Covenanter two years ago,"
another formed about the same distance to the south, and another in
the town of "Carlile" (now "Carlyle") about fifty-five miles away.

By February of the following year, both Bannister and Miller reported that the church was in use.

Randolph Ill, Feb. 18th A.D. 1833

Dear Friend

. . . Our new Meeting House we find quite agreeable. the
building Committee have done themselves honour & although
they had to contend with a strong opposition set by pursuing an
upright course with a firm determination to press on the work
with all convenient speed. The Public now expresses so far as I
know their entire Satisfaction. . . .

Yours with affection

Oliver Bannister

Feb. 1833

We have seen last Sabbath A Beautiful Brick house 60 feet by
45 Completely filled with hearers in a neighbourhood where

12 years ago a house 12 feet Square was Sufficient to contain all
his audience. There is 74 Seats on the floor of the house and they
were all [sold] this Day the highest at 41$ and the lowest at 28.
the Galery will be seated as soon as such a number of Seats can
be sold as will Defray the Expence—the cost so far is 2500$. . . .

Andrew Miller

Squabbles over the new church and over doctrinal differences eventually split the Bethel Church. Oliver Bannister and Andrew Miller,
formerly the best of friends, ruined their friendship over the disagree-
ments that broke the congregation into the "New Lights" and the
"Old Lights." The "Old Lights" continued to follow the strict Covenanter doctrines that allowed no instrumental accompaniment to
their singing or recognition of state or federal governments and encouraged active defiance of state or federal laws they felt were not in
accordance with God's laws. The "New Lights" followed Rev. Wylie
into a more liberal path in regard to church doctrine.

May 5, 1834

Dear Friend,
. . . It is with grief I say A. Miller is no longer considered a man
of Truth. . . . Miller is considered [in] no better light than a
high way robber by all the inhabitants of this county accept
about 6 or 8 old [ones who] will follow right or wrong. . . .
Yours

Oliver Bannister

By the time William and Anna arrived in Randolph County, the
split in the church was complete. The Hayes family joined with the
"Old Lights," thus paving the way for William Hayes to truly live the
articles of his Christian faith.

Letters written in 1841, from family members in both northern Illinois and New York, indicate that William was engaged in something
out of the ordinary.

Stark County, Ill, April 28, 1841

Dear Brother and Sister,

. . . We are well and hope as soon as you receive this you will write and Let us know the reason of your not writing. We think their must be something more than common the matter. . . .

Our love to you all,

H. Hayes (William's sister-in-law)

That "something more than common" is spelled out in a letter from William's brother James.

April 13, 1841

Dear Brother,

. . . I have heard you had trouble for helping the Blacks with a Ride. . . .

Affectionately,

James Hayes

8

The Escape

> [T]he said Defendant . . . unlawfully and unjustly Coun-
> selled, pursuaded, enticed, aided and assisted the said Suky
> so then being the servant of the said plaintiff as last
> aforesaid to run away and absent herself from the service of
> him the said plaintiff.
> —*Borders v. Hayes,* April 14, 1844

Whether or not William Hayes intentionally "pursuaded" Sukey and her family to flee the Borders farm is unclear, but the story told in the trial transcript confirms that he certainly "assisted" her in running away. How she knew about him, or if she knew him personally before she sought his aid, is also a matter of conjecture. No doubt the abolitionists in the area were well known, and perhaps local gossip had transported Hayes's name to Sukey's ears.

Though the route Sukey and Hannah took to reach the Hayes home is unknown, it is likely that they walked on their journey because testimony from John Finley, a neighbor of Hayes, says that Finley spotted a woman and some children walking past the place where he was working. He further stated that he had never seen her in a wagon.[1]

The long walk through the fields and woods separating the Borders and Hayes farm homes must have been a tiring, frightening journey. The creek bed through which they may have walked is bordered by steep banks covered with scraggly trees and thick undergrowth that would have hindered walking with ease. The creek itself is often dry in late summer, but its bed is strewn with stones and rubble. Walking alone in the middle of the night with only Hannah to help with the little ones, hoping against hope that they would find refuge and perhaps a ride to take them far from the master they feared, would have been dreadful.

No doubt a strong impetus for Sukey's flight was the threat to sell her young sons down South. Obviously, she had stayed all those years accepting her lot, despite the horrific conditions, but when her boys were threatened, she took action. She acted as most mothers would have; the safety and well-being of her children were her priorities. William Hayes may have been her only hope to find a new and better life for her family.

For several reasons, Hayes was the ideal man to transport the fugitives to northern Illinois. First of all, the year he spent living near Peoria gave him a thorough knowledge of the land there, and the business contacts he made acquainted him with many people who would be valuable when conducting his illegal activities. Undoubtedly, he knew whom he could trust and whom he could not. In addition, he had relatives living in Knox and Stark Counties. His uncle, Silvanus Ferris, had helped found the city of Galesburg and the Knox Manual Labor College (later known simply as Knox College), and his brother, Harry, after much wandering and indecision, had settled in Stark County. Hayes either knew or was related to several other area residents who helped the women and children after they arrived in Knoxville, the original county seat of Knox County.

Knoxville is located near the center of the county. First known as Henderson Town, and sometimes as Gum Settlement, the post office changed its name to Knoxville in 1837. The focal point of the village was, and still is, a two-story brick courthouse. With large white columns befitting its stature as a seat of county government, it was known in its earliest years as one of the finest courthouses in the state. This imposing courthouse would play a role in testimony given at Hayes's trial.

Usually "conductors" on the Underground Railroad transported their illicit cargo ten miles or so to the next farmhouse in which the owners were known to be sympathetic to slaves. In this case William Hayes proved to be an exception. He took the five Borders servants, probably by wagon, to the Illinois River, where they boarded a steamboat bound for northern Illinois. Although the trial transcript does not state where or when they boarded the steamboat, the two possibilities presented difficulties. They could have driven twenty miles to the Chester Landing, where steamboats made regular stops, but that would have necessitated a change of boats in St. Louis, a town with strong pro-slavery sentiments. The other possibility was a long distance away. Grafton, near Alton, was a likely spot to board boats, but it was more than eighty miles from the Hayes homestead. Since a wagon could travel only twenty miles per day, it would have taken them too long to reach the landing at Grafton and still arrive in northern Illinois five days after the escape.

The most likely scenario places them at the Hayes farmhouse before dawn on September 1, where they could have been hidden until dusk, perhaps in the built-in "box" in the attic of the house. (According to family legend, such a box was used to conceal escaping slaves.) During the night, Hayes could have taken them to the Chester Landing, where, on the following morning, they then boarded a steamboat bound for St. Louis.

Steamboats on the Mississippi traveled at an average rate of ten miles per hour when going upstream; thus it would have taken them a full day to travel the ninety miles to St. Louis. There they would have boarded a packet on the Illinois River. The packet they used is unknown, but it may have been either the *Louisa,* the *Sarah Anne,* or the *Rosalie,* since these boats are known to have been steaming up the Illinois River waters about this time. The first two made one trip a week; the *Rosalie* made two trips each week.[2]

Illinois River steamboats were much more primitive than the ones plying the Mississippi. Described by some as "little more than boilers riding rafts," the first ones on the Illinois had deep hulls and sluggish engines, and disasters were frequent.[3] Recurrent boiler explosions and violent deaths caused steamboat designers to build boats with "drafts of about seven feet or less."[4] Boats on the Illinois traveled more slowly than their sisters on the Mississippi, usually averaging only five miles per hour. The two-hundred-mile trip to Fulton County would have taken about forty hours, perhaps more if they encountered difficulties like sandbars and exploding boilers.

Wherever and however they boarded the steamboat, it is known that they debarked at the "mouth of the Coperas [Copperas] Creek," a heavily wooded area, and they reached Farmington in Fulton County on September 5, 1842.[5]

The *Western Citizen*, a popular antislavery newspaper published in Chicago, carried the first account of the slaves' escape in an unsigned article on September 16, 1842:

> On Monday the 5th instant, two negro women and three
> children arrived at the house of an abolitionist near
> Farmington, on their way to a land of liberty. The negroes said
> that they belonged in the southern part of the State, that they
> were free by the laws of the State, but were claimed by a man
> who had threatened to sell them out of the State to go down
> the river. The people of that section of the country had become
> interested in their case, and had subscribed about $500 to
> defend their liberty in a court of justice; but as their would-be
> master threatened to sell them out of the State, and put his
> threat into execution upon two other negroes—they were
> advised by their friends to follow the North star. On Monday
> in the afternoon they were conveyed by the gentlemen [prob-
> ably including Hayes] above mentioned to the residence of
> another friend, at French Creek, in Peoria co. [Reverend John
> Cross], near the line of Knox County. A Justice of the Peace of
> the latter county [Jacob Knightlinger] understanding that
> negroes had passed that way, collected a gang together, who
> armed themselves and went in pursuit. They overtook the man
> returning, whom they endeavored to stop by threatening to
> shoot him, and by other acts of violence. They next repaired to
> the house where the fugitives had been left, and took them and
> carried them to Knoxville and confined them in jail. On their
> return, they fell in with the Rev. J. Cross, from whose house
> the fugitives had been taken, whom they assaulted and
> stopped, knocking down one of his horses. The next day a
> committee of the friends of the poor fugitives, in Knox County,
> was appointed to consult with legal advisers, and see that
> justice was done to these defenceless women and children. On

Wednesday following, the reputed Justice and some of his gang, were arraigned before N. West Esq., upon complaint of Mr. Cross and the Farmington abolitionist, and the Justice with one of his associates, were fined fifty dollars each.[6]

The Reverend John Cross wrote a "Letter to the Editor" in the next issue of the *Western Citizen*, adding colorful details of the slaves' capture to this rather staid account of the affair. He did this, he said, because "considerable excitement has existed in this region for some days past, and as usual many contradictory reports have been afloat. . . ." He goes on to state that he was gone when the women and children arrived at his home. They had come in an open wagon in broad daylight "without any attempt at concealment." Cross continued: ". . . Messrs. Eli Wilson and E. P. Wilson of Farmington, were passing in a two horse wagon across the prairie, about half a mile from my house when they were forcibly stopped by an armed gang of eight or ten mounted men with rifles and other offensive weapons; who with threats of violence detained them for some minutes, until Wilson's horses by a spirited effort broke through their ranks and galloped off, leaving their pursuers under whip and spur far behind. . . ."[7]

According to Cross, Jacob Knightlinger, a justice of the peace for Knox County, was the head of the gang.[8] The Wilsons demanded to know by what authority they were being stopped, but the gang members produced nothing. The altercation stopped short of gunfire, but only "for fear of killing some of their own party."

The "ruffian gang" then rode to Cross's house, where his wife was home alone with three small children. Cross completes his account with words dripping in sarcasm: ". . . and there with rifles, oaths and threats in terrorem performed the chivalrous and DARING EXPLOIT of capturing two negro women and three children; and conducted them in triumph to the jail of the county at Knoxville. If deeds of she-valory are to be awarded under Captain Tyler's administration; Knightlinger should be made a brevet Major, and Secretary Upshur in his zeal for the 'patriarchal institution,' should present him a wench's petticoat for a banner. . . ."

Cross came home later that evening in the company of a Mr. George F. H. Wilson. They had just reached a spot in the road across from Knightlinger's house when the justice rode up to the side of the wagon, brandishing a rifle, and demanded to know whether or not Cross was in the wagon. When Cross refused to answer, Knightlinger "bawled come on boys, come on!" As he shouted this, the horses pulling Cross's wagon startled and began running at breakneck speed, leaving Knightlinger and his gang far behind. The gang took up the chase, "howling at each leap of their horses like so many prairie wolves." When they reached the home of a David McLaughlin, they were stopped by two or three men brandishing "rails or stakes" who began hitting their horses over the head. McLaughlin tried to shoot his rifle, but it misfired. By this time, Knightlinger had raced up to the group shouting, "Hand them out! Damn them! I'll shoot them!"

Cross demanded to know why they were being stopped but received only threats and curses in reply. Knightlinger's gang proceeded to search the wagon but found "nothing valuable" and so allowed Cross and his companion to leave.

George Wilson complained to Nehemiah West, another justice of the peace, about the altercation, and Knightlinger and McLaughlin were tried and fined one hundred dollars plus costs. Both men appealed the case to the circuit court. Cross adds, somewhat sarcastically, that Knox County residents "will learn whether a jury can be found in Knox county, who will justify such midnight assaults upon the peaceful traveler. If so, all legal protection is gone, and there is no alternative left us under God, but obedience to the prime law of nature to PROTECT OURSELVES."

Knightlinger had his own version of the events, which was published almost forty years later in the *History of Knox County, Illinois*. While his account of what had happened between him and Rev. Cross corroborates Cross's statements to some extent, Knightlinger justifies his actions by insinuating that as justice of the peace, he was only doing his duty to uphold the laws of the state of Illinois when he chased down the fugitives and had them thrown in jail. He further claims that while the case against him, which he had appealed to the circuit court, was thrown out of court by the judge, Rev. Cross was indicted and put in jail. "Afterwards the abolitionists of Galesburg bailed him out. This is all true."[9]

Obviously, feelings ran high in Knox County at this time. "Protecting ourselves" could only mean that the next time such a thing happened, matters would be settled by gunfire.

When the case was appealed to the circuit court the next spring, no witnesses were subpoenaed. Rev. Cross was there voluntarily and was called upon to testify. After his testimony, the court decided that it was "a case of riot, not assault; therefore it was *quashed*."

> . . . The State's Attorney then offered to go with Mr. Cross
> before the Grand Jury and make an effort to obtain a bill of
> indictment for a riot. But Mr. Cross considered this a hopeless
> case, knowing that one of the jury was a principal one to be
> complained of, and how correctly he judged in the case, will
> appear from the fact that this very same jury attempted to find a
> bill against Mr. Cross for perjury, for Testimony given before
> Esq. West! There were those on the jury, however, who would
> not listen to a proposal so unfounded and infamous. Thus the
> case closed.[10]

While all this was going on, Sukey, Hannah, and the three small boys languished in jail "waiting for the arrival of the evidence of their freedom" sought by the appointed Knox County committee.[11] A subcommittee was formed to "see them supplied with all the necessaries and comforts which a miserable jail will permit."

In March 1843 a convention of the Anti-Slavery Society held at Farmington voted to uphold the work of the committee formed in Galesburg not only with their words but also with their pocketbooks. "G. W. Gale proceeded to make a statement of facts [at the Farmington Convention] in relation to the doings of a committee formerly appointed to attend to the case of certain women and children who had been unjustly thrown into jail in Knox Co. The convention voted to sustain that committee in any measures and expenses to procure the liberty of the persons named."[12]

The jail at Knoxville was a bleak affair. Twenty feet square and two stories high, the glorified log cabin stood on the west side of the square, north of the courthouse. It was heated by a fire in the center of the room, which probably did little to keep out the cold prairie winds of early autumn.[13] The fugitives were under the care of Peter Frans, sheriff of Knox County, who immediately advertised throughout the state to find their owner. "Great pains were taken by the sheriff to ascertain the owners of these supposed slaves. Letters were written in different directions. One gentleman came from Missouri in hopes of finding his slaves. In a few weeks a Mr. Andrew Borders, from Randolph Co., Ill., arrived and claimed the mother and three children as his runaway servants."[14]

9

Searching the Cornfields
and Thickets

The cruel treatment which the rest of Borders colored
people received, excited them to seek safety by flight.
They escaped and traveled North, leaving Borders to search
the cornfields and thickets, which he did painfully, for
more than a month, when he heard of them 300 miles
North.

—*Western Citizen*, October 28, 1842

Andrew Borders had been furious when he found his slaves missing. He was still embroiled in a court case over Sarah's escape, and though he had won the first battle, the case had been appealed to the Illinois State Supreme Court and wouldn't be heard until December. Now, having five others flee his farm put him into a rage, and he used his considerable power to hunt them down. The *Western Citizen* told readers exactly how Borders reacted:

> . . . Borders, with his mean and ungenerous accomplices, soon
> became very noisy in blaming the neighbors for secreting his
> slaves. For some time he battered and bullied through the
> neighborhood manifesting the true spirit of a slave holder, used
> to tyranize over his defenceless slaves. The people, who believed
> he had no legal claim in his negroes, did not wish to be insulted
> and trampled upon by this petty tyrant; they entered suit in her
> name for assault and battery, and wages for the time she had
> lived with him. . . .

The suit the writer refers to is the case for Sarah brought by the Friends of Rational Liberty. The purpose of that case was not for her alone but was designed to test the legality of slavery throughout the state or, to use the writer's words, "to reach the ears of all others held in slavery in the state."

Borders felt that he could ill afford to lose six of his "servants," that they were rightfully his property and were necessary in the running of his farm and household. In describing the missing servants to the circuit court in Pinckneyville in 1844, James J. Borders, Andrew's son, stated that Jarrot was nine or ten years old and "fit for right small business." The other children were too young to work, but they represented future earnings for Borders. Young Borders estimated that Jarrot's services were worth five dollars per month "over and above his room and board." Sukey was not used by Borders in his farm operations; rather, she was valuable for her housekeeping services.[1]

About two weeks after the fugitives fled, Andrew Borders learned of their whereabouts and made plans to go to Knoxville to claim them. Accompanied by his son James J., Borders stayed in northern Illinois for "twelve or thirteen days," a trip so expensive that it cost him "about five dollars per day for each."[2] He claimed that Sukey and the boys rightfully belonged to him, but he admitted that Hannah had served her time and was legally free. However, because he had neglected to bring the proper papers with him, the sheriff refused to release the prisoners. While in Knoxville, Borders tried to sell his troublesome chattel to a "colored man" in exchange for a horse.[3] When that plan didn't work, he left town. At the time, the abolitionists in Galesburg thought they had seen the last of him.

William Hayes remained in northern Illinois for several weeks after the fugitives landed in jail, though what he did during this period is unknown. No doubt he was involved with the committee searching for ways to release the women and children. In late September or early October, he returned home by steamboat down the Illinois River to St. Louis, where he was picked up by James McDowell, apparently a friend who often went to St. Louis with Hayes to do marketing. McDowell probably was not a Randolph County resident because his name does not appear on either the 1840 or 1850 census.[4]

McDowell testified that Hayes "has frequently been in the habit of going North ever since he lived in Randolph County" and that he "has relations in the north part of the state." He further stated that Hayes had neither a horse nor a wagon of his own waiting for him in St. Louis, a fact that further supports the theory that he had taken the slaves to the Chester Landing when they escaped. On their way home, they met James J. Borders in Twelve Mile Prairie.

Young Borders, who by most accounts appears to have been a hot-head who spoke first and thought later, began "cussing" at Hayes and accused him of running off his father's servants. Hayes flatly denied the allegation but stated that he thought Borders had no right to hold them. The confrontation between Borders's son and William Hayes seems to have been only verbal.

James J.'s temper is referred to in a letter to Hayes from Nehemiah West, written from Galesburg a few months later, on February 10, 1843: "[Y]oung James Borders while here made such threats about you as would Subject him to fine and imprisonment if the law was informed. Should you be here at the Court where he is to be you might lodge a complaint here where the proof is at hand to convict him."

After arriving back in southern Illinois, Hayes apparently searched Randolph County records to find evidence that the slaves were not properly registered. He may also have made another trip north because the *Western Citizen* reported:

> [A] gentleman to whom the committee had written for informa-
> tion, arrived from Randolph County, with a certificate from the
> acting clerk of Randolph Co., by which it appeared that none of
> the persons claimed by Mr. Borders had been registered, except
> the mother of the children. He also brought an affidavit of
> William Temple, a neighbor of Mr. Borders, taken before John
> Campbell, a justice of the peace for Randolph Co., and who
> certified to the respectability of the witness. Mr. Temple testi-
> fied that he had known Hannah, the colored girl, for seventeen
> or eighteen years, and that she was two years old when he first

knew her, and that the children of Susan were all born in
Randolph Co., Ills.[5]

Despite the affidavits stating that the boys and Hannah were not
registered, the sheriff refused to release any of the fugitives, not even
Hannah, whom Borders admitted "had worked out her time." The reasons he gave for this decision rested on a technicality: Mr. Campbell
was at that time only an "acting" justice of the peace in Randolph
County.

After his return, "the gentleman from Randolph County," almost
certainly William Hayes, sent other affidavits, this time with the
proper clerk's certificate, but despite this evidence—thought by the
abolitionists in Galesburg sufficient proof to free them—Sheriff Peter
Frans continued to hold them in jail.

> All the affidavits made the girl Hannah a year at least older than
> she was said to be. She must therefore have served Mr. Borders
> one year over her time, for which she has received nothing but
> abuse and imprisonment. And Susan [Sukey], who according to
> the record, and the statement of Mr. Borders, had one and a half
> year more to serve, the gentleman from Randolph County wrote
> that it was believed she had served beyond her time, and gentle-
> men who had lived neighbors of Mr. Borders while in the State
> of Georgia, now living in that county, were willing to testify to
> that fact.

At the end of October 1842, the editor of the *Western Citizen* had
received a letter from Eden in Randolph County titled "Is Illinois a
Free State?" The author of the letter, who wrote under the pseudonym
"Honertah," may have been William Hayes. However, since the writer
appears to be a more educated man than Hayes, a better guess as to his
identity would be the Reverend Samuel Wylie, former pastor of the
Covenanter Church in Eden and currently the pastor of the "New
Light" splinter group, which had left the Covenanter Church. The letter invited others to write the *Western Citizen* in order to debate
whether or not Illinois was truly a free state.

When I became a resident of the State of Illinois, I believed that no involuntary servitude could be maintained by the laws thereof, otherwise than by conviction of a crime. But the event of judicial action, in the circuit court of Randolph County, last April, has led me to doubt, whether my belief has been correct [the writer refers here to Sarah's case, which was currently pending on appeal to the Illinois State Supreme Court]. . . . This must be so, otherwise the action of the court is corrupt.[6]

"Honertah's" letter brought a response from "Ben Franklin"; it was printed on November 11, 1842. "Franklin" gives several statistics about slavery in Illinois at the time and uses a dollop of sarcasm to describe the "freedom" in Illinois.

By the census of 1840 it appears that Illinois has set down to her credit 184 slaves; these are not indentured servants, but bona fide slaves. By the census taken by authority of the state, over 400 more persons are returned who have been deprived of their freedom under the name of indentured servants. . . . It would be a tedious task to enumerate all the items of our slave laws—they are familiar to most of the people of the state, yet Illinois is a free state. . . .
. . . Let us all join then to sing the praises of Illinois, the great, the free, and while we do so, let's drive all niggers far away, that we be not contaminated by their complexion, or be made offensive from the odor that is sure to arise from a negro who is free.[7]

The *Western Citizen* kept its readers informed of the latest developments in the affair. By October 7, it reported that the fugitives were free: "They are now out of jail and living in families in Knoxville."[8] The unnamed people with whom they lived were responsible for seeing that they returned to the jail at the "expiration of the six weeks from the time of their seizure when, according to our laws, they are to be hired out from month to month to pay their jail fees."

A letter written on November 29, signed "H.H.K." (perhaps Hiram Huntington Kellogg, president of Knox College), to the *Western Citi-*

zen indicates that the women and children had been offered for hire at the courthouse door upon the expiration of the six weeks for which they were imprisoned. The sale, which was held on November 10, was a failure. Most of those attending did not come to bid; they assembled for the sale because it was a "novel spectacle." For the most part, those attending felt they didn't need to pay the county for unfairly confining the women and children. Finally, though, a bid was made: a paltry fifty cents for the girl Hannah.[9]

For a time, things looked brighter for the women and children. Hannah apparently found work in a neighboring town (probably Galesburg), but Sukey remained in Knoxville, rented a house, and worked as a laundry woman for various families. Jarrot worked in the fields near town, and Sukey left the younger boys at the hotel (possibly John Gum's hotel) while she worked.[10]

Their taste of freedom did not last. On November 24, "the day after she [Sukey] had gone into her house," Borders arrived bearing the proper indenture papers, and he went directly to Sheriff Frans to claim his property.[11] Frans helped him capture the young boys at the hotel, secreted them in a loft at "Mr. Newman's" house (possibly George Newman, the third treasurer of Knox County), and kidnapped Jarrot from the fields before Sukey could warn him.[12] All three boys were thrown back into the Knox County Jail.[13]

The *History of Knox County, Illinois* (1878) picks up the story. Sukey was frantic. She had been washing at the home of Mr. Cole, a Presbyterian minister, when she learned that Borders had come thundering into town.[14] Borders had a theory: "If I can get the children I am not afraid but what the old one will follow."[15] Although Sukey must have wanted to follow her sons, even into captivity, cooler heads prevailed. One of the most active abolitionists of the area, Charles W. Gilbert, arrived at the Cole residence in time to see a grief-stricken Sukey attempting to go after her children. Gilbert persuaded her to don a disguise, using Mrs. Cole's clothes, and he took her by sleigh to Galesburg.

This time Borders made an entirely new claim for the children: "He now demands them his indented apprentices under the poor laws, and exhibited indentures executed in 1839 and 1841 by justices of the peace in and for Randolph Co. This claim being perfectly satisfactory to the sheriff, he delivered over the children to Mr. Borders."[16]

Members of the committee formed to oversee the fugitives weren't as impressed as the sheriff. They believed that the indentures were probably fraudulent, or at least defective, and they began a suit against Borders before the circuit court. The suit was scheduled to be heard the following June.

They also brought another suit against him, this time in Sukey's name. It stated that the children had been "detained without authority," and a warrant was brought against the Borders men for false imprisonment. Borders appeared before A. S. Bergen, Esq., in Galesburg. At that time, Borders claimed he had indentures for the boys, but he refused to let Bergen see them. He was told that if he truly had proper indenture papers, he wouldn't be bothered again until the next session of the circuit court. Again, Borders refused to produce papers validating the legitimacy of his claim. Instead, he immediately left town and headed back to Knoxville. No doubt he hoped to seize the still-imprisoned boys and take them back to Randolph County.

Galesburg abolitionists lost no time waiting to see if this would happen. They issued another warrant for his arrest, sending an officer to pursue the Borders men. Father and son were brought back to Galesburg about nine o'clock on Friday night. They subsequently were found guilty of false imprisonment and fined five hundred dollars, a sum that Sheriff Frans paid.[17]

On Saturday morning, Borders finally turned over the indenture papers that proved he owned the children.[18] The committee, however, found fault with them. Jarrot's papers had a hole where his age should have been, and the others contained erasures not certified by the probate judge of Randolph County. Thus, Borders and his son were again found guilty and were fined four hundred dollars. When they refused to pay, the court ordered them to appear at the next session of the circuit court and sent them to jail—the same jail that held Sukey's children. The jail was described at the time as "a cold, open log jail, with neither stove nor fire-place, with an open vessel only of some kind with fire to warm them, the smoke passing out of the openings on each side of the prison, and this in very inclement weather."

Such accommodations proved "too uncomfortable a place to spend the night," though the jail supposedly was adequate for children. Sheriff Frans made sure the Borders men did not suffer too long in such primitive conditions. He and some unspecified "others" again supplied their bail, and they were released.

The children, though, had disappeared. Who took them, how they were taken, where they went—all remained a mystery that was never satisfactorily explained. The *Western Citizen* stated that "they" had taken the precaution of sending the children off secretly some twenty-four hours before, but it is unclear who "they" were. Implied is the suggestion that Andrew Borders, with the cooperation of Sheriff Frans, was responsible for their removal.

The committee tried to get the children back and offered "reasonable security" that if Borders left them in Knox County, they would bring them on the first day of the circuit court. Borders refused. He offered to sell them, but the committee countered by saying they would pay his legal expenses if he would "relinquish them all." He refused this offer as well.

Sukey remained in Galesburg near despair. But the abolitionists there assured her that she would see her sons again.

IO

Searching the Records

Mr. Gale recd your letter which was the bearer of great
satisfaction to Susan as it allayed her fears about her
children being sold into Slavery. . . . Hannah is with me
going to School and wishes to send to her mother that she
is well.

—Nehemiah West to William Hayes,
Galesburg, Illinois, February 10, 1843

While Sukey, or "Susan" as the abolitionists in Galesburg now
called her, may have been relieved to learn that her sons had
not been sold into slavery, William Hayes's troubles were just beginning. On February 8, 1843, Borders sued him in the Randolph County
Circuit Court for twenty-five hundred dollars, an enormous sum for a
poor dairy farmer.[1] How Borders knew to blame Hayes is unknown,
though the people who helped escaping slaves were probably well
known in the community. At least one, A. Burlinghame, made no effort to conceal his "after hours" activities.[2]

William Hayes knew the letter writer, Nehemiah West, very well.
West had been on the scouting party that came from New York in
1835 searching for a suitable place on which to build a new town—
one that would be far away from the "temptations" that were numerous along the commercial and industrial river towns in the East. A
pious man, West believed that God himself had pointed an all-know-
ing finger to land lying on a level stretch of prairie west of Knoxville.
The soil was black and fertile, lying as it did amid a vast stretch of
prairie unbroken by trees or large streams. The scouting party bought
up thousands of acres of land on which to build their town and the

college they intended to establish, but only 160 acres were set aside for the town itself. The rest was sold in 80-acre increments to those interested in becoming a part of this great experiment.

One member of the scouting party, Silvanus Ferris, was an uncle of William Hayes. While not an official member of the purchasing committee, Ferris's son, Silvanus Western Ferris, most often called simply "Western," wrote to William Hayes in November 1835 telling about the trip to Illinois and the purpose of the expedition.

> St. Louis Missouri November the 9th 1835
>
> Dear Cousin Sir
> . . . The object of our business was to purchase land in the
> first place. The friends of benevealence at the east have associ-
> ated together for the purchase of establishing a literary institu-
> tion in the State of Illinois on a plan which . . . I can . . .
> describe. . . . [I]t was proposed to raise forty thousand dollars
> by subscription and lay out one half of the amount in land at
> government price and the remainder to be applied for other
> purchases such as erecting Colledge buildings & each sub–
> scription was to be 400 dollars and each subscriber to have 80
> acres of land and a schollarship for twenty five years that is
> tuition and room as the institution is on the Manual labor
> system.
>
> I remain your affectionate cousin
>
> Silvanus W. Ferris

The town of Galesburg—named for George Gale, its stern, uncompromising leader—was divided into forty-two blocks. A small town square provided the only attempt at beautification, for the founders believed that beauty and pleasure were sinful. In Galesburg, even the celebration of Christmas was forbidden, and alcoholic drink was an abomination.

Nearly half the residents of the fledgling town were Congregationalists, who spent a great deal of time in worship and prayer. After the Knox Manual Labor College was established, classes were often canceled because of revivals.

Not surprisingly, the pious folk of Galesburg were drawn to the cause of the poor, downtrodden slaves. In the decades immediately prior to the Civil War, the God-fearing residents of Galesburg took an active part in the Underground Railroad. For a time, it was known as "a little island of abolitionism," and it was here that the first antislavery society was founded.[3]

In the letter written February 10, 1843, Nehemiah West[4] asked that Hayes search for proof that Sukey gave her consent for the boys to be indentured, as was required by the Act Concerning Apprentices:

> [T]he law under which he [Borders] holds the children is the third law of an "act concerning apprentices" . . . you will See by that act that there must be the Concent of a parent if their is any. If not a Guardian Certified on the indenture which is wanting. Also there must be an exact copy recorded in the office of the Probate Justice at the date of the same. Now we want you [to] examine that office well and ascertain the fact and whether if it is found it should appear probable that the one was put there in 1837 or has been added Since. . . . Your Search of Records will be Confined to the Probate Office—try to ascertain when and where those indentures and by whom they were written.

Hayes probably found time to search the probate records as West requested. An article in the *Western Citizen* states that "a gentleman to whom the committee had written for information, arrived from Randolph Co." It appeared from the documents this "gentleman" brought with him that "none of the persons claimed by Mr. Borders had been registered, except the mother of the children."[5]

While searching the probate records and still embroiled in the legal controversy with Borders, Hayes apparently continued his work with the Underground Railroad. On February 27, T. A. Jones wrote to inform him about routes that existed to transport slaves to the northern part of the state.

Bond County, Feb. 27, 1843

. . . There is a line from Quincy running through Canton And I expect to go north in the Spring and will do all I can to get one firmly established from your place to meet it either at Canton or above. . . . If you can find any way to get the poor traveller to Capt. Breath's [A. Breath, a representative for the *Western Citizen*] near Marine. They will Send them up to Mr. McCords, Wafers, or Douglass'es. . . . Send on all you can Get to any one of those men and they will be carried safely on. . . .

No record exists to tell us whether or not Hayes used any of these "lines" to the north, particularly at this time, and it seems likely that his pending court case with Borders may have reduced his activity to a minimum.

I I

Preparing for Trial

Received of William Hayes by the hand of Andrew Miller
Twenty five Dollars for legal services rendered.
—L. G. Trumbull to William Hayes,
Belleville, Illinois, November 26, 1844

I n anticipation of the coming trial, Andrew Borders and William
Hayes each chose counsel who were well-known legal celebrities of
the era.

David Jewett Baker, who filed the Plea of Trespass on the Case
against William Hayes at the county seat in Kaskaskia on March 2,
1843, was a fifty-two-year-old native of upstate New York. He immigrated to Kaskaskia as a young man and quickly gained prominence
as a lawyer. While serving as a probate judge of Randolph County,
then-Governor Ninian Edwards appointed him to fill the unexpired
term of Senator McLean in 1830. He served in that capacity for only
thirty days.[1] From 1833 to 1841, he served as United States district
attorney. Curiously, Baker was known as an antislavery advocate; indeed, sources say that "his opposition to the introduction of slavery
into the State was so aggressive that his life was frequently threatened."[2] Even more curious is the fact that he owned one female slave
in 1825, so his beliefs on the slavery issue were questionable at best.[3]
Baker's role in *Borders v. Hayes* would not be a large one, and he never
appeared at the Perry County trial. He did, however, represent Borders at the Illinois State Supreme Court two years later. Borders probably engaged him to fire the first volley in his attack against Hayes
simply because he had a fine reputation as a lawyer and because he

lived in the county seat. Borders hired even more prominent lawyers to try the court case.

Borders selected William Henry Bissell, a thirty-three-year-old Belleville lawyer, to be his lead attorney. By all accounts, Bissell was a rising star in Illinois legal circles. Bright and well educated (he had first graduated from Jefferson Medical School in Philadelphia), Bissell's chief asset was his oratorical power, and he was considered to be one of the best political speakers in the entire state.[4] A charmer who possessed a wry sense of humor, he could also indulge in cutting satire when the occasion warranted.

Though Borders had undoubtedly heard of Bissell's expertise when he served as prosecuting attorney of St. Clair County, another influence may have swayed his decision to engage William Bissell as his legal representative: Bissell's wife was the daughter of his old friend and pro-slavery advocate, Elias Kent Kane, the man who had first owned Sarah and Hannah.[5] Borders and Kane were such close friends that Andrew Borders had named one of his sons Elias in his honor.

Borders chose thirty-five-year-old Gustave Philip Koerner, a fire-brand revolutionary in his native Germany during the Burschenschaft uprising, to round out his team of legal representatives. Koerner had fled Germany in 1833 after he was wounded in the Frankfort revolt and had first settled in Missouri. An outspoken defender of freedom for all people, he quickly moved to St. Clair County in Illinois when he learned that slavery was practiced in Missouri. He wrote in his memoirs: "What we heard here [Lexington, Kentucky, where he attended law school and first saw slavery in practice] and what we saw . . . contributed to our detestation of the institution of slavery and confirmed our determination not to settle in Missouri."[6] Considering the antislavery bent he exhibited from the beginning of his residence in the United States, it is puzzling that Koerner would agree to take a case in which he would have to argue for a slaveholder. It is equally puzzling that Andrew Borders would have wanted such a man as his representative.

William Hayes also chose men of distinction to defend him in his civil trial. Pictures of Lyman Trumbull, the lawyer Hayes chose to act as one of his two attorneys, show a grim-faced man with a receding hairline. Though he possessed a brilliant legal mind and became increasingly active in national politics as the years progressed, one source says that "his colorless public personality denied him the kind of support on which spectacular careers are built."[7] Other sources also speculate on his "coldness," but it was more likely that he was a man of formal dignity who had difficulty in social situations. At the beginning of *Borders v. Hayes*, he was only thirty-one years old, a relatively new bridegroom expecting his first child.[8]

Trumbull's reputation as a fierce opponent of slavery may have influenced Hayes to engage him. Possibly he knew too that Trumbull often fought slavery cases in the lower courts without fees or remuneration, though he didn't work entirely pro bono for William Hayes. Receipts exist testifying that Hayes made payments for his legal defense in this trial amounting to forty-five dollars during the year after the close of the trial.[9] Whether or not this represented his entire legal costs is not known.

William Underwood, who served as Hayes's second counsel, was only twenty-six when Hayes engaged him. Like William Hayes, he had been born in New York State and had moved west to further his opportunities. At the age of twenty-three, he had been elected district attorney in St. Clair County.

For the lawyers involved, the case of *Borders v. Hayes* was just a blip in their careers, for the majority of them went on to serve in important state and national positions. For William Hayes, though, the case was the cataclysmic event of his life.

I 2

Legal Wrangling

[T]he fact of the prejudice of the inhabitants of said
County against him has come to his knowledge since the
commencement of this Court & . . . fears that the same
feeling exists in the County of Monroe as in this County,
therefore he prays that the Venue in this case may be
changed to some County where the causes complained of
do not exist.

—*Borders v. Hayes*, April 28, 1843

On April 28, 1843, the defendant's attorneys asked for a change
of venue because they felt that William could not receive a fair
trial in Randolph County. Hayes and his lawyers believed that residents of the county were prejudiced against him. Stating this may indicate that the case was well known and talked about in Randolph
County.

The change of venue was granted on April 29, 1843, and the case
was moved to Pinckneyville in Perry County.[1] Hayes and his lawyers
probably thought the change of venue would be beneficial to their case
because slavery was nonexistent in Perry County. The census of 1840
reports not a single slave being held in Perry County. Only seven African Americans made their home there, all members of the same family.
Since they were listed as farmers and common laborers and not as servants, they undoubtedly were free.[2] Thus, any jury pool chosen from
the Perry County population presumably would be free of the Southern
prejudice that permeated Randolph County.

Borders, however, had other legal matters to attend to before he
could fix his full attention on his upcoming battle with William

Hayes. On May 9, 1843, Sheriff Peter Frans delivered a summons to Borders to appear in the Knox County Circuit Court to answer to "Hannah (a woman of color,) Of a plea of trespass on the case on promise to the damage the sum of Five hundred dollars."[3] The *Western Citizen* reported that "gentlemen from Randolph County," probably including William Hayes, had arrived and brought "indisputable evidence" to show that Hannah had worked as a field hand more than eighteen months over the time she was indentured, and that she was worth a hundred dollars a year. She had received nothing but "coarse and scanty clothing" for her services.[4] The suit was an attempt to recover at least minimum compensation for the time she had been held illegally as an indentured servant. Again, Borders triumphed. The case was moved from Knox County to Warren County, where it was dismissed in November.[5]

Borders's other Knox County suits came up in May, and the *Western Citizen* again kept readers apprised of the situation. The newspaper stated: "Care had evidently been taken in selecting the jurymen, both petit and grand, to exclude every man who was known to have any sympathy for the slave."[6] Regardless of the nature of the jury, the antislavery faction was doomed to lose that skirmish.

The *Western Citizen* reported that Borders arrived at the Knox County Courthouse with a barrel of peach brandy for "his old friend the Sheriff," and everyone from the jury to the lawyers freely imbibed. Only the judge was excluded from Borders's alcoholic bribe. The case was decided in Borders's favor, and the "petit jury brought in a verdict of 30 dollars damages against the Justice [West] who tried Borders in a suit for detaining his papers from Saturday night till Monday morning." In addition, the paper reported that the litigious atmosphere in Knox County seemed to run rampant: "[T]he grand jury not only found bills of indictment against those who had given food and shelter and clothing to the mother who had been robbed of her clothing, as well as children, by Borders, but whom the sheriff had not even demanded after he sent her off to shift for herself; but they seemed resolved to indict every man who could be indicted under any pretence."

"Under any pretence" covered a lot of territory. One man in Galesburg was charged with wife beating; and the whole school board, trusted with the common schools in town, was charged for mishandling funds. Both suits eventually were dismissed.[7]

Of more importance to the abolitionists in Galesburg were the indictments brought against Rev. John Cross, George Washington Gale, Nehemiah West, Charles Gilbert, and perhaps others for harboring Borders's slaves. Though the suits languished in court much longer than the wife-beating or school funds charges, they eventually amounted to nothing. Charges against Nehemiah West were dropped in November 1843; Gilbert's case was changed to Warren County, where it was never prosecuted; Gale simply refused to show up in court. Eventually, his case was also dismissed. Rev. Cross's case took much longer to resolve, but when it finally came to trial, Andrew Borders did not appear to testify against him. Since his testimony was needed, the state's attorney wanted to continue the case to the next term. Cross thwarted this by admitting his guilt. This so surprised the prosecutor, who was not prepared for the trial, that he entered a motion to dismiss the case, "thus depriving Cross of an opportunity for an anti-slavery lecture by way of an address to the jury."[8]

Back in Randolph County, Hayes prepared for his trial. In an undated letter to his wife, he states: "I now think I will go on with the trial." In this letter he gives Anna instructions regarding people he would like to attend the Perry County proceedings. At the time, he even expected Nehemiah West to come down from Galesburg. It is doubtful that West came, however, since only his deposition is entered into the trial transcript. This undated letter (c. 1844) is one of only two letters written in his hand in the Hayes Collection.

> If Mr. West gets here from the North he can get a horse to
> wride and leave [it] at Barkers and I will settle the Keeping
> and you must get a long as well as you can [at] home till I get
> back. . . .
> Yours
>
> William Hayes

Beginning in the spring of 1843, lawyers on both sides began taking depositions from Knox County residents who would be unable to attend the trial because they lived so far away from Perry County. Borders filed for a deposition to be taken from Sheriff Frans.[9] Defendant Hayes asked for depositions to be taken from George Gale, Frans, and Nehemiah West.[10] William Hayes was preparing for the biggest ordeal of his life.

13

The Trial Begins

The river is high and without Mary Rachel has a good
way of coming with company that Suits her She can if she
thinks best keep out of the way though I think she would
be a help in the case but I will not advise except for her to
stay at home or out of the way.
                    —William Hayes to Anna Hayes, c. 1844

The spring of 1844, or the "wet season" as it was called in southern Illinois, was characterized by drenching rains, severe thun-
derstorms, and high winds. The March "rise" of the rivers, which came
every year, was higher than anyone could remember, and by April,
water threatened the county seat of Kaskaskia. In June, water stood
at the windowsills in Kaskaskia, then plunged into the houses nearest
the rivers. People fled the area, deserting their homes and farms in un-
precedented numbers.

Though the letter Hayes wrote to his wife is undated and does not
have a return address, it seems likely that he wrote it either from
Kaskaskia, where the suit originated, or from Pinckneyville, where the
case would be tried, in the early spring of 1844. The letter, written in
pencil and very difficult to decipher, says that "the witnesses had better
be here by the third Morning," a statement that seems to indicate it
was written from Pinckneyville.

When he wrote the letter, the rivers had begun to rise, but the worst
of the flooding had yet to occur. However, the state of the rivers was
bad enough that he was concerned for his oldest daughter, Mary
Rachel. Even though he thought she might "be a help in the case," he
urged her to remain at home, "out of the way," unless she could find

someone to come with her. It is not known how Mary Rachel could have helped him with his dispute with Andrew Borders.

In any event, Hayes apparently couldn't settle the legal contest without having a trial. Pleas were heard on "the third Monday of April in the year of our Lord 1844" in Pinckneyville, county seat of Perry County. The date was April 15, 1844.[1] The jury reached a verdict on April 18.

Pinckneyville, located twenty miles east of the Hayes homestead in Flat Prairie, had been founded as the county seat of Perry County in 1827. For a few months, the circuit court met in private homes, but in 1828, a log building was erected for use of the court and other county offices. By 1835, the need for a new courthouse was apparent, and plans were made to construct a newer, more modern, building. The second courthouse, the one in which Andrew Borders and William Hayes met in their legal battle, stood on the square, on the same site the current courthouse occupies. It was an imposing building for its time. Built of "brick set on edge," it stood a lofty two stories high. Each story was forty-three feet square and sported "two or three chimneys" leading to open fireplaces on both floors. On the second story, five windows of "twenty-four lights [panes] each" were placed on three sides of the building. The fourth side had two windows that "corresponded to the number of doors and windows below." Outside the courthouse was a holding pen for stray animals that wandered the unpaved streets of the village. Contractor Amos Anderson completed the building in 1837 for a total price of $1,765.[2]

The lawyers who assembled in the Perry County Courthouse on April 15, 1844, were not the only well-known legal celebrities at the trial that day. The judge appointed to hear the case was famous in his own right. The Honorable James Shields, "one of the officiate Justices of the Supreme Court" of Illinois, presided.[3] Shields had been appointed to the supreme court of Illinois just the year before by Governor Ford, but he had been a resident of Kaskaskia since 1823, immigrating to the United States from Ireland. He had cut a wide swath through Illinois since his immigration. He served in the Illinois House of Representatives from 1836 to 1838 and was Democratic auditor for the state from 1841 to 1843, before being appointed to the supreme court of Illinois.

Possessed of a fiery temperament, Shields challenged Abraham Lincoln to a duel in 1842 because he thought Lincoln had written derogatory letters about him that were published in a Springfield newspaper. The two men met to duel with swords as their weapons, but Shields realized that Lincoln's reach far surpassed his, and the confrontation was canceled.[4]

Gustave Koerner knew Shields well because they had been law partners from 1837 to 1841. Though in his *Memoirs* Koerner describes Shields as an extremely egotistical, vain man who was very ambitious and somewhat "peculiar" and "eccentric," he greatly admired him and said "he was my most intimate American friend."[5] William Bissell was also well acquainted with the judge. An 1841 advertisement in the Sparta newspaper attests to that fact.

Shields and Bissell

Attornies and counsellors at law, will practice as partners in the counties of Randolph, Monroe, and St. Clair. One of the partners may at all times be found at their office in Waterloo, Monroe County.[6]

The jury that would decide the case consisted of twelve "good and lawful men": Hampton H. Bourland, James G. Jackson, Jr., Woods A. Hamilton, James Johnson, Richard Williams, John White, Homer Wells, Thomas Brinkley, John Eaton, John G. Moore, John D. Reese, and Peter W. Wilkes.[7] Most were young, married farmers, ranging in age from their early twenties to mid-thirties. All were married men, except for John Moore; Hampton Bourland and John White may have been over the age of fifty; and only John Eaton worked as something other than a farmer. In census records, he is described as a "Minister of Christ of the Universalist Denomination." None were slaveholders, though a few may have been exposed to slavery in their early years. Richard Williams and his wife had come from Kentucky and Tennessee, respectively; John White had lived for a time in South Carolina;

Thomas Brinkley had lived in Kentucky; and Peter Wilkes had originated in Virginia. In addition, John Eaton had been born in Tennessee, John Moore in Kentucky.[8]

The stage was now set. The lawyers assembled with their clients, the judge sat down behind the bench, and the jurors took their seats prepared to hear the testimony that would either prove or disprove the allegations of the plaintiff, Andrew Borders.

14

The Plaintiff's Case

Yet the said Defendant well knowing the premises but
contrary and wrongfully & unjustly intending to injure,
prejudice and aggrive the plaintiff in his aforsaid business
and to deprive him of the services of the said Sucky, Jarrot,
Anderson & Harrison . . . Unlawfully wrongfully &
unjustly aided and assisted the said Sucky, Jarrot, Anderson & Harrison . . . to absent themselves from the service
of him the said plaintiff.
                        —*Borders v. Hayes*, April 14, 1844

Andrew Borders was no stranger to the circuit court in Randolph County. Records indicate that he had been involved in
numerous lawsuits between 1840 and 1845. Usually, he was the plaintiff, but on a few occasions he was the defendant. As plaintiff, he most
often foreclosed on mortgages; as defendant, he had been accused of
destroying a landmark and he had been sued for past wages by the servant girl Hannah.[1] Almost always he emerged the victor in the various
suits in which he was engaged. Undoubtedly, he expected to win his
contest against William Hayes. Besides having a competent team of
lawyers, Borders's wealth and political contacts made him a formidable
foe for anyone who tried to cross him.

In contrast, William Hayes was a novice at legal games. He was not
a wealthy man; he had formed no powerful political allies to aid him.
And he was a religious man who would not employ underhanded tactics in order to win, as Borders had done when he took a wagon load of
peach brandy to the courthouse in Knoxville in his earlier suit in Knox
County. Hayes was definitely vulnerable and ill prepared to take on an

adversary as Herculean as Borders. He had only his belief that he was innocent of wrongdoing in God's eyes, no matter what the prevailing laws might be.

Borders also believed himself to be in the right because his servants were his property, and property was so sacred in the eyes of nineteenth-century men that stealing a man's horse was thought to be more diabolical than swiping his wife. Snatching his servants, who were necessary in the running of his house and farm, was a crime of such magnitude that Borders reacted with a vengeance. He intended to punish Hayes to the full measure of the law.

Andrew Borders v. William Hayes was not a criminal case, however. It was a civil case punishable by fine, not by imprisonment. If awarded, the $2500 fine Borders asked for would have crippled Hayes financially.

Borders presented some justification for the fine he hoped would be imposed on William Hayes. Not only had he been deprived of the services of his slaves, but he had "been put to great trouble, cost and expense" to get them back. These expenses had been incurred when he and his son, James J., traveled to Knox County in order to identify and claim his slaves. Borders estimated that he spent $150 each on getting the boys back and $200 in his failed attempt to get Sukey back on his farm. Though these expenses constituted only $650, Borders asked for $2500 in damages for Hayes's part in the disappearance of his slaves.[2]

After their opening statements, of which there is no record, William Bissell and Gustave Koerner, the plaintiff's attorneys, attempted to admit into evidence the indenture records of Sukey, Jarrot, Anderson, and Harrison that were listed in the Registry of Negroes, Mulattoes &c in the Randolph County records, in order to prove that they were indeed the property of Andrew Borders.

Hayes's lawyers objected strenuously to this because they felt the information was "irrelevant" and didn't prove that Sukey and her sons had been properly registered. Judge Shields overruled their objection, and those papers were read before the jury.

The plaintiff's lawyers called James J. Borders as the first witness to testify in his father's behalf. James J. told how valuable the slaves were to the running of his father's farm and informed the jury about the month-long trip he and his father had made to Knoxville to claim their recalcitrant servants. Their expenses included not only food and lodging for themselves, but a medical bill of five dollars for one of the boys and payment of the prisoners' jail fees.

He mentioned the incident in Twelve Mile Prairie in St. Clair County when he accidentally met Hayes and James McDowell. He accused Hayes of running off his father's slaves. According to his testimony, Hayes refused to comment on his accusations, except to say that the elder Borders had "no title to them."[3]

Borders's lawyers then called Joseph H. Orr, a neighbor who lived four or five miles from Andrew Borders. Orr stated he was well acquainted with the slaves in question. He further testified that the night before the slaves escaped, he had noticed a crowd in the woods near his home, but William Hayes had not been seen. He understood that Hayes had "gone North."

It's difficult to tell why Bissell and Koerner included Mr. Orr's testimony. Certainly, his words established that William Hayes was gone from his home *before* the slaves escaped, a detail that would not have helped the plaintiff's case. Other details are more difficult to decipher. Was the crowd in the woods important to the case? Were they perhaps the abolitionists who called themselves the Friends of Rational Liberty? Did the plaintiff's lawyers believe that some kind of conspiracy lay behind the escape? These questions are impossible to answer more than 150 years later.

David Curry next testified before the jury. Curry, who is not listed in any Randolph County census report, lived about "fifteen yards" from William Hayes's home.[4] Since he lived so near to Hayes, he may have been a hired hand who helped out with the farm work, especially during Hayes's frequent absences from home. Curry said Hayes wasn't home on September 1, 1842, but he had no idea where he had gone. His absence from his family and farm wasn't unusual, though, because Hayes often traveled to the northern part of the state, where he had relatives and where he still conducted business in buying and selling land. He did say that William Hayes told him he had nothing to do with the disappearance of Borders's slaves.

Curry admitted that he knew Jarrot, though he professed ignorance of the other fugitives. Jarrot had come to his house, which was on the Hayes property, one afternoon before the escape, but he did not know "where from nor where he went. Jarrot asked me for nothing and [I] do not know his business." Curry was certain that he'd never seen Jarrot with William Hayes, "at that time or any other."

John Finley took the stand next. His testimony placed the fugitives at William Hayes's home. Early on the morning of September 1, he had seen a black woman about thirty years old walking with two children past the lot where he was working. Later in the day he saw them again—this time at Hayes's house. He said that he and the defendant didn't talk about the woman and her children, and he wasn't acquainted with them.

James McDowell was the next witness called by the plaintiff. McDowell probably was a close friend of William Hayes because he states that he and Hayes often went to St. Louis to market. At the time he met Hayes in St. Louis in the fall of 1842, William Hayes had been gone "some weeks," and the witness had picked him up, since Hayes didn't have a wagon, a statement indicating that William Hayes probably had arrived in St. Louis by steamboat. Throughout his testimony, McDowell stressed that it was not unusual for Hayes to be gone from his farm, nor was it strange for McDowell to pick him up in St. Louis, since he had done that many times in the past.

Other statements indicate that McDowell and Hayes had more than a passing acquaintance. Their friendship had spanned a "number of years," and he was well acquainted not only with Hayes's traveling habits but also with the reasons he usually gave for leaving home for extended periods of time. "[I] have known the defendant a number of years. The Defendant has relations in the brother in Stark County and an Uncle in Knox County. [He] has frequently been in the habit of going North ever since he lived in Randolph County. Used to live north and has been gone nearly if not quite half his time from [his] house since his residence in Randolph County for the last nine or ten years."[5]

McDowell's version of the meeting between James J. and William Hayes in Twelve Mile Prairie is much more colorful than the one given by James J. in his testimony before the court. Where James J. says he "accused" Hayes of running off his father's slaves, McDowell says James J. "began cussing at the Defendant. . . ." According to this witness, Hayes had stated that the "[p]laintiff had no right to the negroes, but denied that he had run them off."

William Bissell and Gustave Koerner concluded the plaintiff's case by presenting depositions from two witnesses who lived in Knox County. Neither of them appeared at the trial because they lived 250 miles away, a distance so great that it would "in all probability be very difficult if not impracticable to procure such . . . attendance."[6]

In the year before the trial began, Borders's lawyers proposed deposing Peter Frans and Sally Newman, who, they said, were material witnesses in the case. Frans (sometimes spelled "France") was a man somewhere in his mid-forties who had eight children ranging in age from "under 5" to early twenties.[7] Sally Newman was probably the wife of George Newman, third treasurer of Knox County. Newman was the mother of a large brood of children, perhaps as many as ten. She and her husband had taken Sukey and her children into their home when they were first released from jail.

Lyman Trumbull and William Underwood objected to these depositions because they were "wholly irrelevant to the matters in issue" and because Hayes had not been notified that the depositions would be taken. In addition, Hayes's lawyers believed that neither Peter Frans nor Sally Newman knew where the slaves had come from. Despite their objections, Judge Shields allowed both depositions to be read before the jury. Hayes's lawyers, or their representatives, would have been allowed to be present when the depositions were taken so that they would have a chance to cross-examine the witnesses, but no record of any cross-examination exists.

Peter Frans's deposition for the plaintiff was taken at the Knox County Courthouse in Knoxville on March 7, 1843, a full year before the trial began.[8] Besides admitting that he knew both Borders and Hayes, the only thing Frans said that implicated William Hayes in the case was "Hayes told me that he had brought the negroes away [and] that he was paid for it [and] that he was not an abolitionist."[9] That statement clearly implicates Hayes, but it is unclear how being paid for helping slaves escape would be in his favor, as Hayes must have believed when he made the statement. Perhaps he thought that being paid for it would imply that he held no strong opinions regarding slavery and that his involvement was purely a business matter. In fact, in the years prior to the Civil War, many people of both races charged exorbitant fees to help escaping fugitives, even if they were not in sympathy with the abolitionists.[10] By telling Frans he was paid to help in their rescue, Hayes may have been trying to refute the belief held by the sheriff and perhaps others that he had intentionally enticed Sukey and the others to flee the Borders farm.

In his deposition, Frans also stated that Jarrot was a mulatto, signifying at least that he was light skinned. Frans explained that Borders claimed Sukey as his own and that the boys "had been given up to . . . Andrew Borders on his paying their jail fees."[11] Borders did not claim Hannah, whose indenture had expired. Frans further declared that Sukey "either ran away or was taken away from my custody, so that Borders did not get her." He claimed he hadn't seen her since then.

Sally Newman's deposition wasn't taken until March 20, 1844, about a month before the trial.[12] Her testimony was much more damaging to Hayes's defense. She stated that she was "some acquainted" with both Borders and Hayes but that she had seen and talked with Hayes when he visited her home while Sukey and her children were living with the Newmans. At the time Hayes visited her, he pulled up a chair and sat by the kitchen door while he told Mrs. Newman that Sukey was a friend whom he had brought up "to the mouth of the Coperras Creek [and] that he came on the same boat with her."[13]

Sukey had not been at home when Hayes visited the house, but he did have a conversation with her "on the way from Mr. Gum's," where she had been when Hayes arrived. Mrs. Newman stated she had no idea what the two had discussed in that conversation.[14] She added that they appeared to know each other well and that Sukey had inquired about the health of his family. She placed his visit sometime in the fall of 1842, after the women and children had been released from jail. Newman herself was illiterate; her deposition was signed with an X.

Thus, the plaintiff's lawyers ended their case. They had entered indenture records into the trial transcript that proved Andrew Borders was the rightful owner of the fugitives in question. They succeeded in establishing that William Hayes was absent from his home in Randolph County at the precise time the slaves escaped, though several witnesses indicated that this was not unusual. John Finley's testimony placed Sukey and at least two of her children at the Hayes farmhouse on the day of the escape.

Borders's attorneys had presented a strong circumstantial case against William Hayes. What possible defense could Lyman Trumbull and William Underwood present that would mitigate the damage done by the testimony of the plaintiff's witnesses?

15

The Defendant's Case

And the said Defendant comes and defends the wrong
and injury . . . and says he is not guilty of the grievances
above laid to his charge or any of in manner and harm as
the said plaintiff hath thereof above complained against
him & of this he puts himself on the county.
—*Borders v. Hayes*, April 14, 1844

William Hayes pled not guilty to the charges brought by Borders,
but he preferred not going to trial at all. Immediately after
Borders filed suit in 1843, Underwood and Trumbull attempted various tactics to get the case dismissed. When their efforts failed, they
sought to block the depositions of Knox County witnesses that might
prove damaging to the case. They were especially worried about the
deposition from Peter Frans, sheriff of Knox County. As early as September 1843, Underwood filed an exception to his deposition, but the
reasons to support the exception seem trivial: "Because the answers to
questions in said deposition are ambiguous in this to wit said Frans
States that said defendant admitted to him that he (Defendant) had
brought the said colored persons away without referring to the place
from which they were brought. From anything in said deposition Defendant may have brought them from another and different place than
Randolph County."[1] The real reason for objecting to Frans's deposition
was that the testimony of the Knox County sheriff pointed an accusing
finger directly at William Hayes.

In like manner, Hayes's lawyers took exception to a deposition taken
from Sally Newman for exactly the same reasons. Perhaps even more

than the Frans deposition, Sally Newman's testimony implicated Hayes. She testified that Sukey and William Hayes had been together during her trip North. The defendant's lawyers failed to eliminate these possibly detrimental witnesses, and their depositions had been read before the court.

In an attempt to neutralize the deposition Peter Frans gave for the plaintiff, Hayes's lawyers took another one from him on June 10, 1843.[2] This deposition gave a much more detailed account of Hayes's activities in Knox County, but whether the lawyers helped his case is open to debate.

Particularly, Underwood and Trumbull sought details about a conversation Frans had with Hayes that had been alluded to in his earlier deposition for the plaintiff.

> *Interrogatory 6th:* Did you testify in that deposition as to a conversation between you and William Hay[e]s and yourself in which conversation you testified that Mr. Hay[e]s said that he brought away the negroes [and] that he was paid for it [and] that he [Hayes] was no more of an Abolitionist than Yourself?
> *Answer:* I think that was about the conversation.[3]

Frans said his conversation with Hayes had taken place on the west side of the steps at the Knox County Courthouse in Knoxville and had continued on the road between Knoxville and Galesburg. He and Hayes were not alone that day. Nathan Olmsted Ferris, a cousin of William Hayes, had also been present. Ferris probably could not have heard any of the conversation between them while traveling the Knoxville/Galesburg road, Frans said, because the parties used two wagons: Ferris rode with Frans in a wagon carrying brick; Hayes and Ferris's son occupied the other one. Sometimes the two wagons were side by side on the road, but at other times they were some distance away from each other.

> *Interrogatory 25th:* Did he say he was not an abolitionist in the conversation on the road between Knoxville and Galesburg?
> *Answer:* I do not recollect that he did.

Interrogatory 26th: Did he say it in the conversation on the road that he took the negroes away?

Answer: I think not.

Interrogatory 27th: Did he say in the conversation on the road that he was paid for taking the negroes away?

Answer: We conversed about the negroes as many as two or three times that day and whether he said that in both places I cannot say, but I think it was at the court House. I am of [the] opinion that it was at both places.[4]

Nathan Olmsted Ferris, most often called by his middle name, was a son of Silvanus Ferris, who was one of the founders of Galesburg and the brother of Mary Ann Ferris Hayes, William Hayes's mother. Ferris was an interesting man in his own right. Described by some as a "jack of all trades," he imported the first flock of sheep to the Galesburg area, and he dabbled in experimental farming, raising such exotic crops as canary birdseed, mustard, and popcorn. When he learned that popcorn was not grown in England, he took twenty barrels to London and gave demonstrations for the likes of Queen Victoria and her husband Albert, the prince consort. His adventurous spirit took him to California during the gold rush of 1849, where he died in an accident.[5]

The defense lawyers included Ferris's deposition, taken September 7, 1843, at the trial.[6] Ferris remembered the conversation on the courthouse steps and the ride to Galesburg a bit differently than Frans.

Interrogatory 3rd: Did you hear the said Hay[e]s in that conversation say to Mr. Frans that he [Hayes] brought the negroes away— that he [Hayes] was paid for it—that he [Hayes] was no more of an Abolitionist than the said Peter Frans—or any words to that effect?

Answer: The words used by Mr. Hay[e]s at that time were addressed to me—He said this man (naming Mr. Frans) thinks that I am rather a bad fellow—but I never have joined the abolitionists and this was all that was said on that subject at that time. . . .

Ferris states that he rode only part of the way to Galesburg in Frans's wagon. The rest of the time he rode in his own wagon with William Hayes. He and Frans had discussed the situation while they rode together, but Hayes could not have heard any of it because the only times the two wagons were together were "when my wagon passed his which was on a round trott."[7]

The deposition of Nehemiah West, taken on June 10, 1843, the same day as the Frans deposition, proved to be the most damaging to William Hayes's case.[8] It is the only one entered into the trial transcript that includes cross-examination questions from the plaintiff. The questions asked during the cross-examination are the ones most detrimental to the defense. Many of them were objected to by the defense lawyers, but since they were included in the transcript, Judge Shields must have overruled them, though no mention of his ruling appears in the official copy of the trial.

Interrogatory 23rd: Are you an abolitionist[?] (Objected to by Deft.)
Answer: I am according to the definition that I give of the word, not the definition that others give.
Interrogatory 24th: Did you ever hear Mr. Hay[e]s speak any thing of these negroes[?]
Answer: I have.
Interrogatory 25th: Well, what did he say[?]
Answer: I do not know where to begin. I have heard him say a great deal about them.
Interrogatory 26th: Did you ever hear Mr. Hay[e]s say any thing about bringing them up[?]
Answer: I never did.
Interrogatory 27th: Do you know how they came up here[?] (premptorily objected to by defendant except as regards the Defendant himself)
Answer: I know nothing about how they got here except from the colored persons themselves—I have heard them say how they got here but never heard from any other person.
Interrogatory (28th) 27th: Well, how did they say they got here[?] (objected to by the Defendant)
Answer: They said they ran away from Mr. Borders and came part of

the way in a wagon—part of the way in a steam boat & part of the way a foot.

Interrogatory (29th) 28th: Did they say who fetched them on the wagon[?] (Objected to by Deft.)

Answer: I should think they named a number of Individuals.

Interrogatory 29th: Did they say that Mr. Hay[e]s fetched them on the wagon[?] (Objected to by defendant)

Answer: I think they said they rode in Mr. Hay[e]s' wagon part of the way.[9]

Nehemiah West had delivered the most injurious testimony of the case. As a close friend whom Hayes had earlier expected to make the 250-mile trip to Perry County for the trial, he had been instrumental in the abolitionists' activities to help the five fugitives, and, as such, he no doubt felt that he, like William Hayes, was doing God's work and obeying God's laws. Being a devout man who took his Christianity seriously was a double-edged sword. Such a man would not perjure himself; such a man would feel duty bound to tell the truth, even if it meant implicating his friend, William Hayes, in the illegal work of the abolitionists.

West also attested to the fact that Borders had tried to rid himself of his troublesome slaves while he was in Knoxville. According to West, Borders had talked to several people, trying to sell them "from one hundred dollars down to 25 dollars."[10] He also attempted to trade them to "Black Joe" for a horse. Apparently, he failed to strike a bargain with anyone.

Underwood and Trumbull included only these three depositions in presenting the defense for Hayes, and they did little to bolster his case before the jury. West's testimony, in particular, pointed the finger of guilt directly at Hayes. No Randolph County witnesses were brought before the court. No local friend, no acquaintance testified in Hayes's behalf. Hayes himself never took the stand in his own defense. A contemporary reader of the trial report can only ask why.

16

The Verdict

The court is requested to instruct the jury in this that if
they believe from 1st the evidence that Deft is guilty as
charged in the said Declaration therein the Plaintiff can
only record in this action the value of the services lost up
to the time of the commencement of this suit and the
reasonable expenses in getting such servants back again
necessarily incurred. 2nd That the jury must believe from
the evidence that the said Suky and her children were
bound under service to said Borders as his apprentices or
servants before they can find a Verdict for the Plaintiff.
—*Borders v. Hayes*, April 14, 1844

With these instructions to the jury, given on behalf of the defendant, Trumbull and Underwood sought to lessen the fine Hayes would have to pay, if indeed he were found guilty. As stated previously, Hayes could not be thrown in jail because this was a civil, not a criminal, suit, but he could be fined a sum that might prove far too expensive for a poor dairy farmer.

William Hayes seemed to be plagued with money troubles throughout his adult life, beginning long before Sukey and the others fled the Borders farm. The year 1841 in particular seemed filled with financial difficulties. On January 11, 1841, he received a notice from Alexander Wylie that unless he and James Crouch paid their debt to him, the matter would be "put in the proper courts of collection." On May 15, I. M. Livingston of the firm of Hungerford & Livingston in St. Louis wrote demanding $649.08 that Hayes and Oliver Bannister owed them, saying "we must have the money without further delay."

The letter does not indicate the goods or services that Hungerford &
Livingston had provided. The following June, F. A. Kent of St. Mary's
Landing demanded immediate payment for some lumber that Hayes
"& others" had ordered.

> St. Mary's Landing June 29, 1841
>
> . . . Your note payable at the Bank of Cairo is deposited with
> that Bank for Collection as you are doubtless aware, and I write
> this merely to inform you that it will become due on the 1st of
> July, & to beg you will let nothing prevent its being promptly
> met, as the disapointment this business has already caused me
> has been a very great injury to me. . . . I trust there will be no
> delay.
>   Respectfully yours
>
>   F. A. Kent

Hayes may have tried to solve his financial difficulties by selling off
his assets. The Hayes Collection contains a printed broadside in which
he offers all that he had at auction:

PUBLIC VENDUE

> THE subscriber, expecting to be from home this winter, and
> having sold his farm, will offer for sale, at public vendue, on
> Friday the 29th of October at 10 o'clock, A.M. at his residence in
> Flat Prairie, his personal property, consisting of 4 horses, 40
> head of cattle, 50 hogs, improved breed, one two horse waggon,
> harness, ploughs, cradles, hay, grain, in the stack, the half of a
> thrashing machine, some lumber, and a variety of other articles
> too numerous to mention. . . .
> October 13, 1841
> William Hay[e]s

Curiously, it is not known whether this sale took place, though it
seems unlikely. The broadside states that his farm "has" been sold, yet
the farm in Flat Prairie remains in the hands of his descendants today.
It is also not known why he decided to sell everything he had. And

why did he "expect to be from home this winter?" Did he intend to move his family elsewhere? If so, why? Was it merely financial problems that led him to advertise all his worldly goods for sale, or was it something else?

William's financial woes continued in 1842. On March 30 he was sued by one John Worth for not paying a debt of $456.31. Hayes freely admitted that he owned Worth the money, and judgment for the debt was found against him complete with damages of $46.03.[1]

William Hayes began selling off land in 1843. In December, with his trial looming for April of 1844, he sold, for $1,950 in gold, 320 acres of land to William Addison, complete with "improvements and crops." Hayes retained the right to remove the "log building to the West of the other building[s] and to have of the use various buildings and offices till April 1844."[2]

He continued trying to raise money in 1844. One month before the trial, he borrowed $500 from Samuel W. Dobbins, using land as collateral. He was bound for a period of three months.[3]

Lawyers for both plaintiff and defendant were allowed to tender jury instructions for the judge to consider, and it is not surprising that Bissell and Koerner had instructions that differed from the defendant's. "And afterwards to wit the said Plaintiff asked the court to instruct the Jury 1st That if the Jury believes from the evidence that said Plaintiff lost the entire services of the registered woman in consequence of the Defendants acts—The Plaintiff is entitled to the Value of the term of her service. 2nd That the Knowledge of the Defendant charged with the Offence of aiding the escape of Servants may be inferred from circumstances and that slight circumstances will be sufficient.[4]

The court refused to instruct the jury with the defendant's instructions and accepted those given by Borders's lawyers. This action paved the way for Trumbull and Underwood to ask for a new trial if the jury's verdict went against them.

Koerner and Bissell wanted the jury to award Andrew Borders $2500, the full amount asked for in the case. They hoped that the circumstantial evidence presented in the case would warrant such a decision.

On April 18, 1844, the jury of "good and lawful men" reached their verdict. "We the Jury find the Defendant Guilty and access the said Plff damage at three hundred Dollars."[5]

Though the amount awarded was not unduly harsh and did no more than cover a portion of Borders's costs in retrieving his slaves, Trumbull and Underwood immediately asked the court to set aside the verdict and entered a motion for a new trial. Their reasons were four-fold: First, they said, the verdict was contrary to law; second, the verdict was contrary to the evidence given at the trial; third, improper testimony was permitted to go to the jury; and finally, they declared, the court "misdirected the jury." In other words, the instructions given to the jury were those recommended by the plaintiff's lawyers, Koerner and Bissell.

The motion for a new trial was argued before the judge in words not recorded in the transcript, but the motion was "overrided." "It is considered by the court that said plaintiff recover against the Deft the said sum of three hundred Dollars so by the Jury aforesaid in form aforesaid assessed and also his proper cost and charges by him about his suit in this expenses."[6]

Trumbull and Underwood were not yet done with the case, and neither was William Hayes. With their motion for a new trial denied, they moved to the next logical step: They appealed for a hearing at the Illinois State Supreme Court.

Judge Shields granted this appeal with one condition: "And the said Defendant by his Counsel prays an appeal to the Supreme Court Ordered that said appeal be allowed upon the said Deft giving bond with Andrew Miller Security in thirty days from the date hereof in the sum of six hundred Dollars."[7]

Legal bills for Hayes continued to mount, and records show that he made payments throughout the rest of 1844. In June he paid $10 to Manning Swift, presumably a Knoxville attorney, for "taking depositions" in his behalf.[8] In August, he paid $20 to a Clinton County lawyer in another case in which he was involved.[9] In September, he paid $300 to the Perry County Circuit Court for "judgment & Costs" in the case of "Andrew Borders vs William Hay[e]s."[10] In October, he paid $12.93 to Henry Bilderback, constable of Randolph County, "in full of

Debt & costs on an Execution in favor of J. M. Morrison and against the said Wm Hayes."[11] In November 1844 he paid his attorney, Lyman Trumbull, $25 for "legal Services rendered."[12]

William Hayes made one more attempt to raise money to cover these expenses and the ones he would incur when the case reached the Illinois State Supreme Court. Immediately after the trial, on April 25, 1844, he mortgaged 120 acres to Elisabeth Herd for $400.[13]

According to the trial transcript, the appeal bond was made on May 18, 1844.[14] The bond was recorded at the Perry County courthouse in Pinckneyville on September 12, 1844.[15]

William Hayes and his lawyers refused to accept the Perry County decision. Now all their hopes were pinned on the Illinois State Supreme Court, which would consider the case in Springfield the following December.

17

The Supreme Court Decision

> I returned from Springfield a few days ago. Before I left,
> your case against Borders was argued in the Supreme Court
> by Baker and Koerner for Borders and by Trumbull and
> myself in your behalf. We had a long and desperate
> struggle, but I am very confident that we will reverse the
> judgment below.
>
> —Wm. H. Underwood to William Hayes,
> Belleville, Illinois, January 1, 1845

What is now called the "Old Capitol" in Springfield, Illinois, had been in use only five years when Lyman Trumbull and William Underwood climbed its steep steps in December of 1844 to appeal the decision in *Borders v. Hayes.* At the time, Springfield was a relative newcomer to affairs of state, since it had been named the state capital only seven years earlier in 1837. Prior to that time, two other towns had served Illinois as state capitals. Kaskaskia in Randolph County had never been intended to be a permanent capital because of its remote and sometimes inaccessible location, but it was used as such from 1818 until 1820, when the seat of state government moved to Vandalia, a town built expressly for that purpose. Seventeen years later Vandalia proved inadequate to the demands of a growing state government, so the capital had moved once again, this time to Springfield.

Springfield, like many towns in the central part of the state, was a comparatively new community. Though settlers had begun putting down roots in the vicinity as early as 1819, the town itself hadn't incorporated until 1832. By 1840 the population had grown so much that Springfield was chartered as a city.

At the time of Hayes's appeal, Abraham Lincoln was an active participant in affairs of state in the first courthouse. It was here that he used the extensive law library, housed in a room adjoining the supreme court chamber, to prepare speeches and legal briefs. It was here that he researched election returns in the secretary of state's office, and it was here that he swapped amusing stories with cronies in the court's library and office.

The Old Capitol in Springfield, a stately sandstone building built in the Greek Revival style so popular in the 1800s, was completed in 1839. For the first time, the state's capital building housed all branches of government; it also had offices for the governor, auditor, secretary of state, treasurer, and superintendent of public instruction. In addition, both houses of the General Assembly and the Illinois State Supreme Court met there. At the time Trumbull and Underwood went to Springfield to appeal Hayes's case, the courthouse not only was the scene of affairs of state but also served as a civic center of sorts, hosting such community activities as dances, concerts, levees, political rallies, and conventions.

The supreme court chamber was housed on the first floor of the courthouse. Today, after being renovated in the 1960s to look as it had when Lincoln strode the halls of the building, it has that sterile look of a place unused, almost too tidy to have been the scene of lawyers arguing their cases before the group of nine judges who made up the supreme court. With a little imagination, though, the contemporary visitor can visualize how it looked when papers cluttered the desks and voices raised in debate as lawyers from all over the state came to argue their cases before the highest court in Illinois.

A black iron, wood-burning stove sat in the center of the room, near the doors leading into the chamber. On both sides of the stove, simple wooden spectator benches faced the raised dais, where the judges sat. The dais itself was separated from the rest of the courtroom by a curved walnut balustrade that lent an air of formality to the room. In front of the benches, a long table covered in green baize looked toward the dais, which was flanked at the back with red velvet curtains trimmed with gold. An American flag and an eagle on a standard reminded on-lookers and lawyers alike that this was the place where justice was meted out in accordance with the laws of the state and the nation. A stately grandfather clock, a walnut writing desk under a wall of win-dows, and several glass-enclosed bookcases completed the chamber's furnishings.

The room was lit by candles placed in a massive brass chandelier hung in the center of the room, and brass sconces holding candles adorned the walls. Whale oil lamps sat on tables and desks to provide lighting for the supreme court justices and the lawyers who assembled to argue their various cases.

At the time of Hayes's appeal, nine justices sat on the Illinois State Supreme Court, but that had not always been the case. When the state formed in 1818, only four judges, all elected by both houses of the General Assembly, filled those positions. For the first eight years of the state's existence, supreme court judges also served as judges of the cir-cuit courts in the four judicial districts that divided the state.[1] Throughout the years, until 1840, the number of judicial districts gradually increased until there were nine in the state. Dissatisfaction with the court system erupted in 1840 and caused an increase in the number of justices serving on the court. The root of the discontent was primarily political.

In the early years of statehood, Whigs had dominated state politics, but in the ensuing years Whig power decreased while Democratic power surged. The court, however, had remained static. Three justices were Whigs; only one was a Democrat. The "act reorganizing the judi-ciary of Illinois" in 1841 placed five more judges on the court—all Democrats.

The nine judges who sat on the bench the day Trumbull and Underwood argued Hayes's appeal were Chief Justice William Wilson, Thomas C. Browne, Samuel D. Lockwood, Samuel H. Treat, Walter B. Scates, Richard M. Young, Jesse B. Thomas, John D. Caton, and James Shields. Shields, of course, had been the presiding judge at Hayes's Perry County trial.

The justices were a diverse lot. None of them were Illinois natives, as would be expected, since Illinois had been a state for a mere twenty-six years. Eight of the nine had been born and raised in other parts of the country; James Shields had immigrated from Ireland at a young age and received his education in this country.

William Wilson had served as a member of the court since its inception. When appointed as chief justice in 1825, he had been a youthful thirty-one years old.

Most of the justices had backgrounds in the southern states; only Lockwood, Caton, and Treat qualified as certified "Yorkers," all originating in New York State. Caton, however, had had a grandfather who owned slaves in Virginia.[2] Of the nine, Browne and Thomas were avowed pro-slavery advocates. Indeed, Jesse B. Thomas had been a slaverholder early in the century. He owned two slaves in 1810, three in 1818, and five in 1820.[3] It was he who would write the supreme court opinion on Hayes's appeal.

Of the nine justices, only Samuel D. Lockwood was outspoken in his denunciation of slavery. He not only had been vocal before and during the controversial 1824 constitutional convention that attempted to legalize slavery in Illinois but also had served as editor of the *Illinois Intelligencer*, in Shawneetown, when its pro-slavery owner became mired in financial difficulties. Governor Coles had turned the reins over to Lockwood, thereby gaining another newspaper to espouse anti-slavery sentiments.[4]

A year after his death Lockwood was described as follows: "In every place where he resided in the State his influence has been indeed a strong, steady, and reliable power for good, always on the side of freedom, temperance, morality, and the main spring of them all—Christianity."[5]

Lyman Trumbull and William Underwood believed they had just cause to ask that the Perry County decision in the Hayes case be overturned. They began their appeal by setting forth the primary reasons the supreme court should do so.

As is the custom with most appeals, Underwood and Trumbull threw in anything they could think of in order to get the Perry County decision overturned. Many of their arguments were examples of hairsplitting they probably knew wouldn't get the job done. For example, their first objection dealt with a pleading issue: The papers hadn't been filed in the correct manner. Essentially, they claimed that one of the charges against Hayes was a misjoinder. This means that Borders's lawyers had connected charges against Hayes that, by law, shouldn't have been linked together. One claim was for a penalty on a statute; the other was based on common law. (Laws based in "common law" are those not founded on specific legislation.) Today, such a reason for appeal would receive little or no consideration, but in the nineteenth century there were very strict rules on pleading. At that time, it was not appropriate for certain charges to be joined together. This technicality was hastily dismissed by Justice Thomas when he wrote the supreme court opinion.

Another inconsequential item cited by Hayes's lawyers concerned whether or not Sukey had been a "poor child" when she was indentured in 1816. Trumbull and Underwood argued that the term "poor child" should have been used in Sukey's indenture papers, but it did not appear there. Again, Justice Thomas, writing for the supreme court, waved off this issue as insignificant. Though the term "poor child" hadn't been used in the indenture, he wrote, it was logical to assume she had been unable to support herself at the time because she was only five years old.

Underwood and Trumbull also objected to the admissibility of depositions taken from Sheriff Peter Frans and Sally Newman because their place of residence wasn't specifically stated in the depositions. In addition, the attorneys for Hayes claimed that insufficient notice had been given as to where and when the depositions would be taken. Again the supreme court decided this was a technicality too trivial to address.

Another point of contention concerned the measure of damages that were determined. According to Borders's lawyers, Andrew Borders was entitled to the full term of Sukey's loss. Hayes's lawyers wanted Judge Shields to submit an instruction to the Perry County jury that Borders could receive damages only up to the time of the suit and the reasonable expenses necessary to get her back; instead Judge Shields gave the jury instructions that favored the plaintiff. In a January 1, 1845, letter to Hayes, Underwood wrote: "We produced law in a case like this, that the master of Sukey could not recover the value of her whole term of service before it expired. Judge Shields instructed the jury below the contrary."

Last of the inconsequential issues, Underwood believed that Judge Shields had given improper instructions to the jury and should have granted Hayes a new trial, a standard objection still used today, with as little effect as it had on the supreme court in 1844. Judge Thomas summarily dispensed with this too.

The real basis for the appeal hinged not on these technicalities but on a question concerning the court of common pleas, which Underwood mentioned in the same New Year's Day letter: "On a careful examination we found that the old Court of Common pleas was abolished four years before the time Sukey was registered, and her registry was of course a nullity. . . . We had also decisions that the indentures of the children were not binding on them and that they are void also."

Sukey had been registered under the old court of common pleas, and these courts had been abolished. Therefore, said Hayes's attorneys, her indenture had never been valid. "The certified copy of what purported to be a registry of one of said servants was improperly admitted in evidence, said registry, not being in accordance of the territorial laws, not properly certified. . . . The court of common pleas was abolished in 1814, and before the time of said registry; hence a copy of a record of the clerk of that court in 1817 is a nullity."

The court of common pleas dealt with "common law" issues, for example, trespass and breach of contract, and had been used early in the nineteenth century. Criminal cases were never tried in the court of common pleas, only civil actions. However, when Illinois restructured its court system in 1814, the courts for civil and criminal cases were combined into one. Accordingly, Underwood and Trumbull argued that since the court of common pleas no longer existed in 1817, Sukey's indenture could not have been legal.

Jesse B. Thomas, who wrote the supreme court decision, did legal handstands to address this issue, so much so that the decision seems predestined. Word after word, paragraph after paragraph, page after page, he strained to create a logical progression of thought in order to uphold the Perry County decision. He gave a lengthy dissertation about the Indiana territorial laws (of which Illinois had been a part), stating that nothing had been repealed when the Illinois Territory formed and, therefore, the old territorial laws were still good law. He asked rhetorical questions, trying to appear logical.

Did Thomas harbor a predisposition regarding the outcome of this case? This may well have been true, since he was a known slaveholder, at least in the earlier years of statehood. The final decision of the appeal was short and to the point:

> For the deposition of the others [objections raised by Trumbull and Underwood] it will be sufficient . . . to say that it was proved on the trial by the confessions of the appellant and other testimony, making out an irrefragable [irrefutable] chain of positive and circumstantial proof that he [Hayes] was knowingly and wilfully guilty of the wrongful acts charged upon him by the appellee [Borders] in his declaration, and consequently the verdict was neither against the law nor the evidence. The court properly refused to grant a new trial.
>
> The judgment is affirmed with costs.[6]

Judge Samuel Lockwood wrote a brief dissent. Because of his known antislavery stand, it is possible that he also had a predisposition regarding the outcome of the appeal. However, rather than taking numerous pages to present his dissent, Lockwood arrived at his conclusion in a timely manner: "I do not concur in the opinion just delivered. I think that the registry of a servant before the clerk of the court of common pleas, after the court of common pleas had been abolished, was void. I am also of opinion that the registry is void, because of the uncertainty as to the age of the servant attempted to be registered."[7]

William Hayes had lost the final round in this legal skirmish, but the defeat did little to dampen his conviction that slavery was a moral wrong and a blight upon a nation that called itself Christian.

18

The Tale Ends

Our Rail Road in this part of the State is doing but litle
business this Season—I am glad Yours is so prosperous.
—A. S. Bergen to William Hayes,
Galesburg, Illinois, April 7, 1845

Though his defeat in the courts had been a thorough rout,
William's allegiance to abolitionist causes did not diminish. He
continued to be active in the Underground Railroad after his Perry
County trial and supreme court hearing ended. The letter from A. S.
Bergen from Galesburg attests to the fact that his interest, if not his
actual involvement, had not faded.

This letter is the only one in the Hayes Collection written in
Bergen's hand, but this doesn't mean that he was an insignificant
player in the dramatic events that had unfolded in Knox County three
years earlier. He was an active participant in the Borders affair and had
been indicted in 1843, along with George Gale and the others, for harboring the Borders servants.[1]

In his letter, Bergen stated that he had some clothing, sent from
Boston by "the Ladies" that could be used by the abolitionists in
Randolph County, even though "[i]t is not generally as good as it
aught to be to come So far. Still it is well worth the transportation &
three times more, Mostly Second handed." Because the "Rail Road" in
Knox County had not been very busy, he and "Sgt. West" [Nehemiah
West, whose deposition had been read at the Perry County trial] decided that it would be of more use if they sent it to Hayes to be used
"for Northern travelers."

However, Bergen wasn't prepared to foot the cost of the freight bill,
which amounted to $6.62, to southern Illinois. He requested that

Hayes, or perhaps some of his friends, pay all or part of it. He said that if Hayes sent him the money and the name of the person to whom the box of clothing should be addressed in St. Louis, he would send it immediately. Or, if Hayes had a pending trip planned to Knox County, he could pick up the clothing at that time. What Hayes did about this is unknown.

Of more interest to William Hayes was news of Sukey and Hannah, which Bergen included in the letter. "Susan is Well. Hannah also is improving in Education quite fast. Don't you think Susans litle boys are in danger of being run off by the vile hands laid upon those two men lately reported from Your county—cant Something be done to Secure them."

The mention of Sukey's children appears to indicate that they were back in Randolph County, but their safety still seemed to be in question. What the "vile hands" had done to the "two men" is unknown.

A brief mention of one of Sukey's sons was made in the *Western Citizen* in April 1844. "One of those children whom he [Borders] stole from the mother in Knoxville, was recently killed in his horse-mill. Borders has made a great many abolitionists."[2] The child killed in the mill accident had to have been Jarrot, since he was the only one old enough to be working at the mill.

Evidence exists that William Hayes took part in other legal battles involving runaway slaves in the years after his trials. On April 7, 1846, *The People v. William Hayes & Daniel Morrison* took place in Clinton County. The two men had been arrested and indicted for "Harboring a Slave."[3] This case was a criminal, not civil, trial, and it carried the possibility of jail.

No transcript of this trial exists, but mention of it is made in the Clinton County Courthouse records throughout 1846–1849. "The People" were represented by State's Attorney William H. Bissell, the man who had been attorney for Borders in the earlier Perry County trial. The jury trial, held April 7, 1846, found Hayes and Morrison guilty as charged. As usual, the defendants' counsel, in this case William Underwood and Benjamin Bond, entered a motion for a new trial.[4]

Two days later, on April 9, when the motion for a new trial was considered, Hayes "being three times solemnly called came not but made default." So the court ordered that the motion be forfeited and that a scire facias (a writ that compels the defendant to appear in court) be issued against Hayes. The case was continued until the next term.[5]

The People v. William Hayes and Daniel Morrison was next considered on Tuesday, May 11, 1847, and this time neither man appeared in court. A second writ was issued to compel them to return to court, and a writ to arrest Hayes was also issued.[6]

Why Hayes did not appear in court is a mystery, though hints are given in a letter from his brother, James, written from Galway, New York, in December of 1848. In that letter James said he had heard "that you are unwell," and he urged William to write back immediately "of your health in Particular."

On May 18, 1848, Daniel Morrison alone was tried in another jury trial in Clinton County, but Hayes apparently was in attendance because the record book states: "And now at this time comes the said William Hayes unpleaded, with Daniel Morrison who alone is on trial." At this trial Philip B. Fouke was state's attorney, and William Bissell was Daniel Morrison's attorney.[7] It is not known why William Bissell was first the attorney for the prosecution, then changed to become the attorney for the defendant.

Once more the jury found the defendant guilty, and once more his attorney entered a motion for a new trial. This time a new trial was granted.

The case didn't come up again until the May term in 1849. "And now at this time comes the people by their attorney Philip B. Fouke and it appearing to the court that one of the defendants since the last term of this court had died, it is ordered that this cause be dismissed."[8]

William Hayes, dead at the age of fifty-four, had escaped another fine, or possible imprisonment. He left a forty-nine-year-old widow and three children still living at home: Isaac, nineteen; Jane Ann, seventeen; and William James, seven.[9] The cause of his death is unknown.

19

A Legacy of Shame

The Indian War in Florida & the Abolition Speeches in Congress are now our greatest sources of uneasiness—& of the two, I think there is far more danger in the latter to the country at large. But although the work of the Abolitionists may be slow & gradual, yet it will I fear, eventually prove to be ruinous & fatal to the Union of the States.

—James Brown to William Hayes,
Washington City, July 4, 1836

James Brown from Springfield probably served as an aide to William May, a member of Congress from 1834 to 1839.[1] Brown's letters to William from "Washington City" were primarily about a debt he owed Hayes for some land in northern Illinois, but sometimes he ended them with jotted postscripts he called "News" in which he commented on the subjects being discussed in the nation's capital. As early as 1836 he realized, as many feared, that the continuing agitation about slavery might destroy the Union.

The path that William trod in defense of the slave did not die with him. Illinois continued to be a highly divided state even beyond the war that Brown predicted. Though references to the Underground Railroad do not appear in letters to the Hayes family that arrived after his death, abolitionists all over the state persevered in their efforts to improve the lives of those held in bondage.

The road to better conditions for African Americans in Illinois was a slow and tortured one because the white population, especially those in the southern counties, were determined to maintain the status quo.

Though the result of the 1824 constitutional convention election de-creed that slaveholding was banned in Illinois forever, the institution of slavery continued to be recognized in Illinois by the National Census until 1840.[2] Even then, blacks were strictly confined to "their place."

Education of African Americans was a primary source of contro-versy well into the nineteenth century, and in some southern coun-ties, including Randolph, it continued into the mid-twentieth cen-tury. Prevailing opinion in the early 1800s was that black children, even those who were "free," should not be educated at all. When an act establishing common schools in the state passed the legislature in 1825, it provided only for educating white children. Even white mas-ters were forbidden to educate their indentured servants until 1845. The law forbidding education of black children remained in force un-til 1872.[3]

The dispute over the education of black children persisted into the twentieth century, when separate schools were established for black children in many parts of southern Illinois. Schools in Sparta were offi-cially separated by race in 1912, when the Vernon School was built for that purpose. Prior to that a "colored" school was held at the African Methodist Episcopal (AME) Church around 1870. Vernon School ceased operation in 1963, several years after the U.S. Supreme Court integrated the nation's schools with its 1954 landmark decision in *Brown v. the Board of Education of Topeka.*

In the years immediately following William's death, abolitionists increased their agitation to repeal the "Black Laws" of Illinois. The legislature not only ignored their letters of petition, but they moved to make the laws even more stringent. In 1853 John A. Logan intro-duced a bill in the Illinois House of Representatives to make it a crime to bring any person of color into the state—a crime punishable by a fine from one hundred to five hundred dollars. Furthermore, it stated that any such African American would be subject to arrest. The bill passed both the Illinois House and Senate. A few days before the vote was taken the legislature voted overwhelmingly *not* to repeal the Black Laws.[4]

These actions by the state legislature were, of course, a great blow to the abolitionists and their cause. While the Act of 1853 was unpopular with an outspoken press, the majority of Illinois residents remained either unconcerned about the injustices in the system or were strongly in favor of more and more restrictive laws that would impinge on the rights of all African Americans. The Act of 1853 remained the law of the state until 1865.[5]

A constitutional convention was held in 1862. Among the proposed changes in the constitution of Illinois were these articles:

Sec. 1   "No Negro or Mulatto shall migrate or settle in this State, after the adoption of the Constitution."

Sec. 2   "No Negro or Mulatto shall have the right of suffrage or hold any office in this State."

Sec. 3   "The General Assembly shall pass all laws necessary to carry into effect the provisions of this article."[6]

The popular vote defeated the constitution of 1862, but in an independent vote, the majority cast their ballots in favor of these three sections concerning "Negroes." Obviously, the attitude of most white residents had not changed despite the agitation of the abolitionists and a civil war that emancipated all African Americans in the country.

After the Civil War, things gradually improved for African Americans in the northern and central parts of Illinois. However, in southern counties like Randolph, persistent racial problems permeate society even today. It is a legacy of shame that haunts men and women of conscience, even as it haunted William Hayes more than 150 years ago.

Afterword

Yours of July 25th is this day received and in answer I will
say that if I purchase of you, I am willing to pay as much
as I can afford for the claim and perhaps more than any
other person would pay. [I] will give $50 for it provided
you can give me a proper conveyance from a person, or
parties having a lawful right to sell.

—S. H. Mattison to Anna Hayes,
Saratoga Springs, New York, August 9, 1849

By not writing a will, William left his family in a financial predica-
ment. A few months after his death, his widow Anna made at-
tempts to raise cash for her and the children's needs. For example, she
apparently wrote a letter to S. H. Mattison in Saratoga Springs, New
York, trying to sell him some land (the matter is referred to in his letter to her). Without a will, though, she could not sell any of the land
she owned as her husband's heir until his estate was settled.

Mattison alluded to this difficulty later in his letter when he wrote:
"I presume it will be difficult for you to sell and give a proper release of
the claim, unless there is an executor." Mattison, though, had a plan to
circumvent the law in order to make the sale possible: "If you cannot
lawfully convey perhaps the better way will be (in case your deed is not
of record) to get Mr. Rogers to [convey it] to me. This will not be
strictly lawful, but as you only have a doubtful claim it will not be very
material."

Anna and the children probably were not penniless, however, because her half sisters, Jane and Leah Cownover, still lived in the Hayes
household. Jane owned a large amount of land in her own right. In ad-

dition, William and Anna's son, Isaac, was nineteen and of an age to earn the family living.

William's estate, which was not settled in probate until July of 1852, was valued at $182.80. Anna had turned over the office of administrator to their friend, Sam McClinton, a month after her husband's death. A note she wrote, still on file at the Randolph County Courthouse, says: "I heir by re linguish mi right to administor on mi hisband astate to Saml McClinton and no one else."[1] This only known example of any writing done by Anna Hayes seems to indicate that she, like so many other women of the day, was poorly educated. Among her husband's effects were dozens of antislavery books, almanacs, and pamphlets, mute evidence that the abolitionist cause remained close to his heart.

A puzzling letter from Western Ferris mentions a judgment against Hayes that was still outstanding in 1856.

> Galesburg, Aug. 25, 1856
>
> Dear Cousins
> . . . In regard to the Settleing the judgment with B. [Borders] you neede not do anything about it as I have been thinking & getting a little advise on the [subject] & think if you are all still, it will be as well all round as it has been so long since it [was] got. . . .
>   I Remain yours Truly,
>
>   S. W. Ferris

The "judgment with Borders" could not refer to the Perry County trial because a receipt for payment exists. This letter seems to indicate that Hayes owed Borders even more money. What it was for and the amount owed is unknown. Since a receipt from the Perry County Court exists, it is not known what other monies Hayes may have owed Andrew Borders. Ferris writes of a plan to sell some more property, probably in an attempt to raise more cash. By this time, William's estate had been settled for four years, but selling off any land would still be difficult if Hayes still owed Borders money. If indeed Borders hadn't received enough money, a lien would have been placed against any property held by Anna and her children. The plan Ferris advised involved not only Anna but her children, some of whom were now married. In essence he advised her to take the deed for the land and have all the heirs sign off on it, then take it to the county clerk in Chester. He recommended that they take a justice of the peace in their "Waggen" and spend half a day going around to all the heirs for their signatures. The need for secrecy was paramount.

> You can do all this without any one knowing anything about it & Send the Deed to me by Mail. If you had rather put the Deed in some other P. O. than yours you can put it in at your County Seat when the clirk fixes it. You do this, & I will Send you the first Payment as soon as it is done. My lawer thinks that this plan will be the Safest for you & as well for me & Say Nothing to B [Borders] at all. . . .
>
> The way I have proposed is the safest plan for you & the only plan that can be persude [pursued] with Safty & it will satisfy [illegible name] in regard A. B [Andrew Borders]. . . .

One more mention of this affair was made in a letter written by Anna's sister-in-law, Harriet Hayes, in 1857.

> Stark County, Ill April 11, 1857
>
> . . . I think that Ferris did not want the Deed to put on record but to keep it from being on record as a quit-claim from the rest of the heirs would make the title good except Isaac's one share. If you should go up there [Galesburg] and not come this way, get the deed and all the other papers and take them home where they belong. . . .
>
> H. Hayes

Anna Hayes lived three years after this letter was written, dying in 1860, at the age of sixty. In the intervening years since William's death, three of her children had died—Mary Rachel (Elliott) died in May 1857; Jane Ann (Matthews) and William James both died in August 1860.[2] Anna and William had previously lost five other children, most of them at an early age. Of the ten (and perhaps eleven) children Anna bore, only two were living when she died: Margaret Euphame and Isaac Henry.

Andrew Borders lived for fifteen years after William's death, dying in January of 1864, at the age of seventy-one.[3] His wife Martha preceded him in death by three years.[4] In contrast to the paucity of William's estate, Borders left his heirs an estate of approximately $56,155. At the time he was one of the largest landholders in Randolph County.[5]

Of all the players in the drama that took place so long ago, only Sukey and Hannah were living in 1878, when the *History of Knox County, Illinois* was published. The death dates of these two women are unknown.

Unfortunately, Sukey never saw her sons again. Other than the newspaper article stating that one of them had been killed in a mill accident, no trace of them remains. She apparently remained in Galesburg, where she built a new life for herself. She probably married—her surname changed to "Richardson" at some time after she arrived in Knox County. In addition, she may have had more children—the *History of Knox County, Illinois* mentions that while helping another fugitive escape, she locked her house and "with her family as usual went to church," leaving the fugitive at home.[6] At the time the *History of Knox County, Illinois* was written, she was described as "a very intelligent, fine-looking and active old negro lady."[7]

Sukey shed her slave name in the North and was now called Susan in official papers, though she became known as "Aunt Sukey" in the Galesburg area. She spent her last years as a legally free woman. On May 1, 1845, she received her certificate of freedom in the Randolph County Court. Also given her freedom that day was "Matilda Morrison;" she may have been Hannah's mother, whose name was previously recorded as "Sarah Morrison."[8]

Hannah continued her fight with Andrew Borders. Finally, on April 29, 1846, after months of delay in her effort to reclaim the past wages due her, she received a jury trial. However, this case too illustrates the power wielded by Andrew Borders. The twelve white men who served on the jury found in his favor, thus ending any hopes of vindication

Hannah might have hoped for.[9] The final note about Hannah Morrison, made in the *History of Knox County, Illinois,* is that she was living in New York City in 1878.[10]

Most of the attorneys involved in *Borders v. Hayes* became important in the politics of the state and nation. William Bissell realized his early potential by becoming the first Republican governor of Illinois in 1856. His colleague, Gustave Koerner, who served as lieutenant governor during the administration of Governor Joel Matteson, became increasingly involved in the antislavery movement as it became an issue of national importance in the years prior to the Civil War. As a close friend of Abraham Lincoln, he assumed some of Lincoln's cases in Springfield and was consulted on matters Lincoln deemed important. Because Koerner was a staunch Union supporter during the War Between the States, Lincoln rewarded him with the post of minister to Spain in 1862.[11]

Lyman Trumbull, who represented William Hayes early in his career, served as a United States senator in the era marked with bitter struggle over slavery and reconstruction after the Civil War. He was one of only seven who voted against impeaching Andrew Johnson. His most distinguished achievement, however, was writing the Thirteenth Amendment to the United States Constitution, the amendment that ended the legality of slavery nationwide.[12] Though Trumbull and Koerner were opponents in *Borders v. Hayes,* the two men actually were such close friends that Trumbull spoke the eulogy when Koerner died in 1896.[13]

The other lawyer representing Hayes was William Underwood. Two years after the trial, he was elected a state senator. As senator, he was known as an extremely conscientious member who never missed a session or committee meeting.[14] He enjoyed a long and successful career but never rose to national importance.

James Shields, the supreme court justice who presided over the Perry County trial, became prominent in national government. He has the distinction of being the only man who ever served in the United States Senate from three states (Illinois, Minnesota, and Missouri).[15]

Thus, more than 150 years ago, the curtain rang down on a well-publicized case that has remained part of the folklore of the Galesburg area. For the first time, though, the southern portion of the story has been revealed to more than just the descendants of the William Hayes family.

The tale was passed down through generations of the Hayes family accompanied by the feeling that their ancestor's part in the affair should remain secret. They felt that it was a blight on the family name that one of their own had been a known lawbreaker. With the passage of time, however, these feelings of shame have been diluted, and William Hayes's involvement in the affair has become a source of pride.

NOTES

BIBLIOGRAPHY

INDEX

NOTES

All letters cited are from a private collection of the papers of William Hayes. The author's transcript of the letters contained in the Hayes Collection can be found at the Sparta Public Library in Sparta, Illinois, and in the Knox College Library in Galesburg, Illinois.

I. SUKEY

1. Hermann R. Muelder, *Fighters for Freedom: A History of Anti-Slavery Activities of Men and Women Associated with Knox College* (New York: Columbia University Press, 1959), 205.
2. *Sarah, alias Sarah Borders, a woman of color v. Andrew Borders*, in J. Young Scammon, *Reports of Cases Argued and Determined in the Supreme Court of the State of Illinois* (Chicago: Callaghan & Co., 1886), 4:355 (hereafter cited as *Borders v. Borders*).
3. Matthew Chambers and his wife, Nancy, lived in T5S, R5W in Randolph County (see *Index to the 1850 Census of Randolph County, Illinois* [Yakima, Wash.: Yakima Valley Genealogical Society, 1976], 1). Another Matthew Chambers lived in Knox County, where he was elected president of the first Anti-Slavery Society in the winter of 1838–1939. Because the suit originated in Randolph County, it is likely that the Randolph County Matthew Chambers is the one referred to in the suit (see Muelder, 68, 74n, 100n, 136, 142, 166, 167n, 380; *Matthew Chambers v. The People of the State of Illinois*, in Scammon, 4:364–72 [hereafter cited as *Chambers v. The People*]).
4. *The People v. Matthew Chambers*, Randolph County Circuit Court, Record Book B., 97, Randolph County Courthouse, Chester, Ill.
5. *Chambers v. The People*, 372.
6. *Borders v. Borders*, 354; Muelder, 206.
7. *Combined History of Randolph, Monroe, and Perry Counties, Illinois* (Phila-

delphia: J. L. McDonough & Co., 1883), 107 (hereafter cited as *Combined History*); Norman Dwight Harris, *The History of Negro Servitude in Illinois, and of the Slavery Agitation in That State, 1719–1864* (1904; Ann Arbor, Mich.: University Microfilms, 1968), 1–2. Harris writes that "landowners were left unmolested in the management of their estates; and the question of the treatment of servants was very seldom if ever raised."

8. E. J. Montague, *A Directory, Business Mirror, and Historical Sketches of Randolph County* (Alton, Ill.: Courier Steam Book & Job Printing House, 1859), 22.

9. "Petition for Slavery in Kaskaskia and Cahokia," *Journal of the Illinois State Historical Society* 47 (1954): 95.

10. *Andrew Borders v. William Hayes* (hereafter cited as *Borders v. Hayes*), Perry County Circuit Court Trial Transcript, April 18, 1844, 21–25. Hayes Collection.

11. *Borders v. Hayes*, 21–25. Hayes Collection.

12. *Borders v. Hayes*, 27. Hayes Collection.

13. *Borders v. Hayes*, 6. Hayes Collection.

2. THE MAJOR

1. *Borders v. Hayes*, 39. Hayes Collection.

2. C. Edward Skeen, "'The Year Without a Summer': A Historical View," *Journal of the Early Republic* 1 (Spring 1981): 51–67.

3. Charles M. Wilson, "The Year Without a Summer," *American History Illustrated* (June 5, 1970): 26.

4. Skeen, 57.

5. Skeen, 63.

6. *Combined History*, 384.

7. Original Land Patent Record, 32B, Randolph County Courthouse, Chester, Ill. Borders's original land purchase lay in sec. 4, T5, R6.

8. *State of Illinois Archives Division Public Domain Sales Land Tract Record Listing,* Springfield, Ill., 22869. Borders's second land purchase lay in Randolph County, sec. 4, T5S, R6N and sec. 34, T4S, R6W.

9. Harris, 6–7.

10. Harris, 8.

11. Harris, 9–10; *Combined History*, 120; Thomas Ford, *A History of Illinois*

from Its Commencement as a State in 1818 to 1847 (Chicago: S. C. Griggs & Co., 1854), 32–34.

12. Christiana Holmes Tillson, *A Woman's Story of Pioneer Illinois,* ed. Milo Milton Quaife (Carbondale: Southern Illinois University Press, 1980), 141.

13. Newton Bateman and Paul Selby, eds, *Historical Encyclopedia of Illinois* (1902; Astoria, Ill.: Stevens Publishing Co., 1970), 483.

14. *Sparta Democrat,* 16 April 1841.

15. *Sparta Democrat,* 26 October 1840.

16. *Census of Randolph County, 1825,* comp. Mrs. Harlin B. Taylor (Decatur, Ill.: Vio-lin Enterprises, 1972), 8, 20.

17. *Census of Randolph County, 1825,* 3; *Borders v. Borders,* 343. Andrew Borders acquired Sarah and Hannah on May 5, 1825.

3. A DIVIDED COUNTY

1. Paul Simon, *Freedom's Champion: Elijah Lovejoy* (Carbondale: Southern Illinois University Press, 1994), 118–35; Horace White, *The Life of Lyman Trumbull* (Boston: Houghton Mifflin Co., 1913), 8–10. Though not an eyewitness, Trumbull's letter to his father, written a few days after Lovejoy's murder, is one of the few contemporary accounts.

2. *Western Citizen,* 23 March 1843, front page, col. 1.

3. *The Sparta Herald,* 20 March 1840.

4. *The Sparta Herald,* 3 April 1840.

5. W. E. B. Du Bois, *Black Reconstruction in America, 1860–1880* (New York: Atheneum, 1975), 145–49.

6. *Western Citizen,* 2 March 1843, p. 126, col. 5.

7. David Ray Wilcox, "The Reformed Presbyterian Church and the AntiSlavery Movement," (Ph.D. diss., Colorado State College of Education at Greeley, 1948), 72.

8. *Sparta Democrat,* 30 November 1841.

4. A GREAT UNDERTAKING

1. Richard J. Jensen, *Illinois: A Bicentennial History* (New York: W. W. Norton & Co., Inc., 1978), 12–13.

2. Montague, 179–80.
3. Montague, 153–58.

5. THE "JURNEY"

1. Laurie McCarthy Talkington, *The Illinois River: Working for Our State* (Champaign: State of Illinois Office of Publications Services, 1998), 3; James Ayars, *The Illinois River* (New York: Holt, Rinehart & Winston, 1968), 32.
2. Bateman and Selby (Chicago: Munsell Publishing Co., 1902), 419.
3. George Flower and Morris Birkbeck, *History of the English Settlement in Edwards County Illinois, Founded in 1817 and 1818.* (1882; Ann Arbor, Mich.: University Microfilms, 1968), 179. Though the prairie described in this account is not in Randolph County, Flower's and Birkbeck's descriptions would have been applicable to any prairie in the state.
4. One popular guidebook to the Illinois Country was J. M. Peck, *A Gazetteer of Illinois in Three Parts* (Philadelphia: Grigg & Elliott, 1837).
5. Senator J. M. Robinson. Letter to the People of Illinois, 3 March 1840.
6. *State of Illinois Archives Division Public Domain Sales Land Tract Record Listing,* 22971. Hayes's land lay in sec. 31, T4S, R5W.

6. NEXT NEIGHBOURS

1. *Census of Randolph County, 1825,* 20ff.

7. THE COVENANTERS

1. Ford, 25.
2. Theodore Calvin Pease, *The Frontier State, 1818–1848* (Urbana: University of Illinois Press, 1918), 69.
3. Wilcox, 54.
4. David M. Carson, "The Reformed Presbyterian Church of North America: A History," in *Psalm Singing of the Covenanters,* ed. Peter Lippincott (University City, Mo.: Prairie Schooner Records, 1977), 24.
5. David M. Carson, "The Reformed Presbyterian Church and Slavery," *Covenanter Witness* (February 1994): 5–6; Wilcox, 114.

6. Pease, 375.
7. "Is It Scriptural: Instrumental Music in Religious Worship," *The Reformed Presbyterian Witness and Missionary Advocate* (February 1902): 41–44.
8. *Combined History*, 243–44; Wilcox, 89.

8. THE ESCAPE

1. *Borders v. Hayes*, 42.
2. "The Importance of Steamboats," *Journal of the Illinois State Historical Society* 47 (1954): 427.
3. Larry Underwood, "The Passing of an Era," *Outdoor Illinois* (February 1975): 8.
4. Eleanor Bussell, "Steamboats on the Illinois River," *Outdoor Illinois* (December 1970): 25.
5. *Borders v. Hayes*, 19–20; *Western Citizen*, 16 September 1842, p. 30, col. 6; Peck, 184. Peck states that Copperas Creek "rises near Canton, runs a southeastern course, and enters the Illinois river in six north, five east. Much of it is a timbered tract; some good prairie, and a large settlement."
6. *Western Citizen*, 16 September 1842, p. 30, col. 6.
7. *Western Citizen*, 23 September 1842, p. 34, col. 4.
8. Knightlinger's name is spelled "Kitlinger" in the *Census of Knox County, 1840*, 149. According to the census, he was a man in his mid-thirties.
9. *History of Knox County, Illinois*, 213–15.
10. *Western Citizen*, 6 April 1843, p. 145, cols. 3–5.
11. *Western Citizen*, 23 September 1842, p. 34, col. 4.
12. *Western Citizen*, 23 March 1843, p. 137, col. 1.
13. The old log jail was replaced by a brick building that was completed in 1845 (see *History of Knox County, Illinois*, 140, 145).
14. *Western Citizen*, 6 April 1843, p. 145, cols. 3–5.

9. SEARCHING THE CORNFIELDS AND THICKETS

1. *Borders v. Hayes*, 40.
2. *Borders v. Hayes*, 40.
3. *Western Citizen*, 6 April 1843, p. 145, cols. 2–3.

4. *Borders v. Hayes*, 42.

5. *Western Citizen*, 6 April 1843, p. 145, cols. 2–3.

6. *Western Citizen*, 28 October 1842, p. 54, col. 3.

7. *Western Citizen*, 11 November 1842, p. 62, col. 4.

8. *Western Citizen*, 7 October 1842, p. 42, col. 6.

9. *Western Citizen*, 23 December 1842, p. 86, cols. 2–3; 6 April 1843, p. 145, cols. 2–3.

10. *Western Citizen*, 6 April 1843, p. 145, cols. 2–3; *History of Knox County, Illinois*, 205.

11. *Western Citizen*, 23 December 1842, p. 86, cols. 2–3; 6 April 1843, p. 145, cols. 2–3.

12. *History of Knox County, Illinois*, 205.

13. *History of Knox County, Illinois*, 206; Muelder, 211.

14. *History of Knox County, Illinois*, 205.

15. *History of Knox County, Illinois*, 206.

16. *Western Citizen*, 23 December 1842, p. 86, cols. 2–3.

17. *Western Citizen*, 6 April 1843, p. 145, col. 4.

18. *Western Citizen*, 6 April 1843, p. 145, col. 4; Muelder, 211–12.

10. SEARCHING THE RECORDS

1. *Borders v. Hayes*, 1.

2. Burlinghame's house, still standing in Eden, has long been known in Randolph County as "The Underground Railroad House." It is privately owned.

3. Earnest Elmo Calkins, *They Broke the Prairie* (Urbana: University of Illinois Press, 1989), 224; *History of Knox County, Illinois*, 623–31; Lowell A. Dearinger, "Galesburg, the Prairie Colony," *Outdoor Illinois* (October 1968): 8–22.

4. West, a native New Yorker, moved with his family to Log City, outside the proposed city of Galesburg, in May 1836. He was a member of the first board of trustees for Knox College. His home served as a station on the Underground Railroad, and he was the secretary of the first antislavery convention "in this part of the state." West died on February 17, 1847, at the age of forty-six (see Jeriah Bonham, *Fifty Years' Recollections with Observations and Reflections on Historical Events, Giving Sketches of Emi-*

nent Citizens—*Their Lives and Public Services* (Peoria, Ill.: J. W. Franks & Sons, 1883), 521–24.
5. *Western Citizen,* 6 April 1843, p. 145, col. 3.

II. PREPARING FOR TRIAL

1. John Clayton, *The Illinois Fact Book and Historical Almanac, 1673–1968* (Carbondale: Southern Illinois University Press, 1970), 98.
2. Bateman and Selby, 32.
3. *Census of Randolph County, 1825,* 3.
4. Gustave Koerner, *Memoirs of Gustave Koerner, 1809–1896* (Cedar Rapids, Iowa: Torch Press, 1909), 489.
5. Allen Johnson, ed., *Dictionary of American Biography* (New York: Charles Scribner's Sons, 1927), 302.
6. Koerner, 284.
7. Johnson, 20.
8. White, 15–16.
9. Receipts from Trumbull to Hayes, November 26, 1844; Underwood to Hayes, January 18, 1845; Trumbull to Hayes, April 25, 1845; and Underwood to Hayes, April 28, 1845. Hayes Collection.

12. LEGAL WRANGLING

1. *Borders v. Hayes,* 12; Randolph County Circuit Court, Record Book B, 160.
2. *Census of Perry County, 1840* (microfilm M-432, Reel 124, C. E. Brehm Memorial Library, Mt. Vernon, Ill.).
3. *Hannah (a Woman of Color) v. Andrew Borders,* Case No. 191, November 9, 1843, Warren County Circuit Court Records, Box 7, Warren County Courthouse, Monmouth, Ill. The summons for Borders was issued by John G. Sanburn, clerk of the circuit court at Knoxville. There is a discrepancy in the dates given in the summons. The summons was issued on June 9, but the Sheriff says it was delivered on May 9.
4. *Western Citizen,* 6 July 1843, p. 198, cols. 4–5.
5. *Hannah (a Woman of Color) v. Andrew Borders.*
6. *Western Citizen,* 6 July 1843, p. 198, col. 4.

7. Muelder, 213.
8. Muelder, 217; *Western Citizen,* 18 July 1844; *History of Knox County, Illinois,* 213.
9. *Borders v. Hayes,* 1, 11.
10. *Borders v. Hayes,* 11. For reasons unknown, the deposition from Gale was never taken.

13. THE TRIAL BEGINS

1. *Borders v. Hayes,* 1.
2. *Combined History,* 170.
3. *Borders v. Hayes,* 1. For more information on James Shields, see Clayton, 103, 105; Koerner, 414–18; Alvin Louis Nebelsick, *A History of Belleville* (Belleville, Ill.: Township High School & Junior College, 1951), 62, 70.
4. Ruth Painter Randall, *The Courtship of Mr. Lincoln* (Boston: Little, Brown & Co., 1957), 183–91; Peggy Bradbury, "Smallpox Island," *St. Louis Post-Dispatch,* 12 February 1997, sec. E, pp. 1–3. According to most accounts, two of the letters that upset Shields were probably written by Lincoln's fiancee, Mary Todd, and a friend, even though Lincoln reportedly apologized for them. Lincoln is generally acknowledged as the writer of the "Rebecca" letter.
5. Koerner, 414, 415, 417.
6. *Sparta Democrat,* 9 April 1841.
7. *Borders v. Hayes,* 38.
8. *Census of Perry County, 1850,* comp. Maxine E. Wormer (Thomson, Ill.: Heritage House, 1973) (microfilm M-432, Reel 124, pp. 13, 20, 21, 35, 36, 40, 44, 47, 112).

14. THE PLAINTIFF'S CASE

1. Randolph County Circuit Court, Record Book B, 318, 344.
2. *Borders v. Hayes,* 4–9. The trial transcript is somewhat confusing about how much Borders spent in trying to get his servants back. In one place it is stated that he spent $200 trying to get the three boys back and $200 to get Sukey back. Later, it states that it cost him $150 for each boy.

3. *Borders v. Hayes,* 40–41.
4. *Borders v. Hayes,* 41.
5. *Borders v. Hayes,* 42.
6. *Borders v. Hayes,* 11.
7. *Census of Knox County, 1840* (microfilm M-704, Reel 62, p. 95. C. E. Brehm Memorial Library, Mt. Vernon, Ill.).
8. *Borders v. Hayes,* 15.
9. *Borders v. Hayes,* 17.
10. Larry Gara, *The Liberty Line: The Legend of the Underground Railroad* (Lexington: University of Kentucky Press, 1961), 56.
11. *Borders v. Hayes,* 15.
12. *Borders v. Hayes,* 18.
13. *Borders v. Hayes,* 19.
14. *Borders v. Hayes,* 20. Mr. Gum ran the hotel where Sukey may have left her children while she worked.

15. THE DEFENDANT'S CASE

1. *Borders v. Hayes,* 13.
2. *Borders v. Hayes,* 28. Borders had been notified that depositions would be taken for the defendant from Peter Frans, Nehemiah West, and George Gale. Depositions appear in the trial transcript from Frans and West, but not from Gale. It is not known whether or not Gale had a deposition taken.
3. *Borders v. Hayes,* 29.
4. *Borders v. Hayes,* 31.
5. Calkins, 156–58.
6. *Borders v. Hayes,* 36.
7. *Borders v. Hayes,* 37.
8. *Borders v. Hayes,* 31.
9. *Borders v. Hayes,* 34–35.
10. *Borders v. Hayes,* 33.

16. THE VERDICT

1. *John Worth v. William Hayes,* Randolph County Circuit Court, Record Book B, 39.

2. Bill of Sale between Hayes and William Addison, December 26, 1843. Hayes Collection. This sale is recorded January 5, 1844, in Record Book U, Deed Records, Randolph County Clerk's Office, Chester, Ill.
3. Legal document between Hayes and Samuel W. Dobbins, witnessed by James P. Wylie, March 9, 1844. Hayes Collection.
4. *Borders v. Hayes,* 38.
5. *Borders v. Hayes,* 38.
6. *Borders v. Hayes,* 39.
7. *Borders v. Hayes,* 39.
8. Receipt from Manning Swift, June 19, 1844. Hayes Collection.
9. Receipt from Ben Boyd, August 29, 1844. Hayes Collection.
10. Receipt from Perry County Circuit Court, September 8, 1844. Hayes Collection.
11. Receipt from Henry Bilderback, October 7, 1844. Hayes Collection.
12. Receipt from L. G. Trumbull, November 26, 1844. Hayes Collection.
13. The land Hayes mortgaged was "the North half of the NE quarter of Section 31 and the NW quarter of the NW quarter of Section 32." All of it lay in Township 4 South of Range 5 West. It was mortgaged for 10 percent interest per year and was repaid in full on March 7, 1849. This sale is recorded in Record Book U, Deed Records, Randolph County Clerk's Office, Chester, Ill.
14. *Borders v. Hayes,* 44.
15. *Borders v. Hayes,* 45.

17. THE SUPREME COURT DECISION

1. Clayton, 324.
2. Wayne C. Townley, *Two Judges of Ottawa* (Carbondale: Egypt Book House, 1948), 29.
3. John D. Barnhart, "The Southern Influence in the Formation of Illinois," *Journal of the Illinois State Historical Society,* 32, no. 3 (September 1939): 368.
4. Harris, 42, 47.
5. *The Biographical Encyclopaedia of Illinois of the Nineteenth Century* (Philadelphia: Galaxy Publishing Co., 1875), 398 (hereafter cited as *Biographical Encyclopaedia*).
6. *Hay{e}s v. Borders,* in Gilman, Charles, *Reports of Cases Argued and Deter-*

mined in the Supreme Court of the State of Illinois (Chicago: Callaghan & Co., 1886), 1:46–69.

7. *Hay{e}s v. Borders,* in Gilman, 1:45–69.

18. THE TALE ENDS

1. *Western Citizen,* 22 April 1846; Muelder, 249.
2. *Western Citizen,* 13 April 1844, p. 158, cols. 5–6.
3. *The People v. William Hayes and Daniel Morrison,* April 7, 1846, Clinton County Circuit Court, Record Book C, 160, Clinton County Courthouse, Carlyle, Ill. (hereafter cited as *People v. Hayes and Morrison*).
4. *People v. Hayes and Morrison,* Record Book C, 160.
5. *People v. Hayes and Morrison,* Record Book C, 182.
6. *People v. Hayes and Morrison,* Record Book C, 212, 242.
7. *People v. Hayes and Morrison,* Record Book C, 271.
8. *People v. Hayes and Morrison,* Record Book C, 318.
9. Johnston Family Bible, owned by Mrs. Russel Hayes, Sparta, Ill.

19. A LEGACY OF SHAME

1. *Illinois Biographical Dictionary* (St. Clair Shores, Mich.: Somerset Publishers, 1998), 116.
2. Bateman and Selby, 483.
3. Harris, 229, 233.
4. Harris, 236.
5. Harris, 237–38.
6. Harris, 238.

AFTERWORD

1. Randolph County Circuit Court Records, Box 46, Randolph County Courthouse, Chester, Ill.
2. Johnston Family Bible.
3. *Combined History,* 384.
4. Union Cemetery gravestone, Randolph County, Ill.

5. Randolph County Circuit Court Records, Box 9, Randolph County Courthouse, Chester, Ill.

6. *History of Knox County, Illinois,* 209.

7. *History of Knox County, Illinois,* 206.

8. Randolph County Circuit Court, Record Book B, 316.

9. Randolph County Circuit Court, Record Book B, 378.

10. *History of Knox County, Illinois,* 206.

11. *Illinois Historical and Statistical* (Chicago: Fergus Printing Co., 1892), 37; Johnson, 496; Clayton, 103.

12. Johnson, 20; Harris, 123ff; Allan Carpenter, *Illinois: Land of Lincoln* (Chicago: Children's Press, 1968), 71. The Thirteenth Amendment says: "Neither slavery nor involuntary servitude, except as punishment for crime whereof the party shall have been duly convicted, shall exist within the United States, or any place subject to their jurisdiction." Illinois was the first state to ratify this amendment, putting an end forever to the legality of slavery.

13. White, 418.

14. Nebelsick, 71; *Biographical Encyclopaedia,* 276.

15. Clayton, 101.

BIBLIOGRAPHY

Alvord, Clarence. *The Illinois Country, 1673–1818.* Urbana: University of Illinois Press, 1920.

American Slavery as It Is: Testimony of a Thousand Witnesses. New York: American Anti-Slavery Society, 1839.

Andrew Borders v. William Hayes, 1844. Perry County Circuit Court Trial Transcript, April 18, 1844. Hayes Collection.

Ayars, James. *The Illinois River.* New York: Holt, Rinehard & Winston, 1968.

Barnhart, John D. "The Southern Influence in the Formation of Illinois." *Journal of the Illinois State Historical Society* 32, no. 3 (September 1939): 358–78.

Bateman, Newton, and Paul Selby, eds. *Historical Encyclopedia of Illinois.* Chicago: Munsell Publishing Co., 1902; Astoria, Ill.: Stevens Publishing Co., 1970.

Biographical Dictionary of the United States Congress, 1774–1898. U.S. Government Printing Office, 1989.

Biographical Encyclopaedia of Illinois of the Nineteenth Century. Philadelphia: Galaxy Publishing Co., 1875.

Birkbeck, Morris. *Letters from Illinois.* London: Taylor & Hessey, 1818.

Birney, James G. *The American Churches: The Bulwarks of American Slavery.* 3d ed. Concord, N.H.: Parker Pillsbury, 1885.

Boggess, Arthur C. *The Settlement of Illinois.* Chicago: Chicago Historical Society, 1908.

Bonham, Jeriah. *Fifty Years' Recollections with Observations and Reflections on Historical Events, Giving Sketches of Eminent Citizens—Their Lives and Public Services.* Peoria, Ill.: J. W. Franks & Sons, 1883.

Bradbury, Peggy. "Smallpox Island." *St. Louis Post-Dispatch,* 12 February 1997, sec. E: 1.

Buck, Solon J. *Illinois in 1818.* 2d ed. Urbana: University of Illinois Press, 1967.

Bussell, Eleanor. "Steamboats on the Illinois River." *Outdoor Illinois* (December 1970): 25–26.

Calkins, Earnest Elmo. *They Broke the Prairie.* Urbana: University of Illinois Press, 1937, 1989.

Carpenter, Allan. *Illinois: Land of Lincoln.* Chicago: Children's Press, 1968.

Carson, David M. "The Reformed Presbyterian Church and Slavery." *Covenanter Witness* (February 1994): 5–6.

————. "The Reformed Presbyterian Church of North America: A History." In *Psalm Singing of the Covenanters,* ed. Peter Lippincott. University City, Mo.: Prairie Schooner Records, 1977.

Census of Knox County, 1840. Microfilm, M-704, Reel 62, p. 95. C. E. Brehm Memorial Library, Mt. Vernon, Ill.

Census of Perry County, 1850. Comp. Maxine E. Wormer. Thomson, Ill.: Heritage House, 1973.

Census of Randolph County, Ill., 1825. Comp. Mrs. Harlin B. Taylor. Decatur, Ill.: Violin Enterprises, 1972.

Clayton, John. *The Illinois Fact Book and Historical Almanac, 1673–1968.* Carbondale: Southern Illinois University Press, 1970.

Coit, Margaret. *The Sweep Westward: The Life History of the United States, 1829–1849.* New York: Time-Life Books, 1963.

Combined History of Randolph, Monroe, and Perry Counties, Illinois. Philadelphia: J. L. McDonough & Co., 1883.

Dearinger, Lowell A. "Galesburg, the Prairie Colony." *Outdoor Illinois* (October 1968): 8–22.

Dillon, Merton L. "Abolitionism Comes to Illinois." *Journal of the Illinois State Historical Society* 53 (1960): 389–403.

————. "Sources of Early Antislavery Thought in Illinois." *Journal of the Illinois State Historical Society* 50 (1957): 36–50.

Du Bois, W. E. B. *Black Reconstruction in America, 1860–1880.* New York: Atheneum, 1975.

Dunn, Violet. *Saratoga County Heritage.* Saratoga Springs, N.Y., 1974.

Engelke, Georgia. *The Great American Bottom.* St. Louis: C. Sarne Corp., 1893.

Faragher, John Mack. *Sugar Creek: Life on the Illinois Prairie.* New Haven: Yale University Press, 1986.

Fergus, Robert. *Biographical Sketch of John Dean Caton.* Chicago: Fergus Printing Co., 1882.

Flower, George, and Morris Birkbeck. *History of the English Settlement in*

Edwards County, Illinois, Founded in 1817 and 1818. 1882. Ann Arbor, Mich.: University Microfilms, 1968.

Ford, Thomas. *A History of Illinois from Its Commencement as a State in 1818 to 1847.* Chicago: S. C. Griggs & Co., 1854.

Gara, Larry. *The Liberty Line: The Legend of the Underground Railroad.* Lexington: University of Kentucky Press, 1961.

Gilman, Charles. *Reports of Cases Argued and Determined in the Supreme Court of the State of Illinois.* Vol. 1. Chicago: Callaghan & Co., 1886.

Gould, E. W. *Fifty Years on the Mississippi.* 1889. Columbus, Ohio: Long's College Book Co., 1951.

Hannah (A Woman of Color) v. Andrew Borders, 1843. Case No. 191. Warren County Circuit Court Records, Box 7. Warren County Courthouse, Monmouth, Ill.

Harris, Norman Dwight. *The History of Negro Servitude in Illinois, and of the Slavery Agitation in that State, 1719–1864.* 1904. Ann Arbor, Mich.: University Microfilms, 1968.

Hayes Collection. Trans. Carol Pirtle. Sparta Public Library, Sparta, Ill.; Knox College Library, Galesburg, Ill.

History of Knox County, Illinois. Chicago: Charles C. Chapman & Co., 1878.

Hosmer, William. *Slavery and the Church.* New York: William J. Moses, 1853.

Illinois Biographical Dictionary. St. Clair Shores, Mich.: Somerset Publishers, 1998.

Illinois Historical and Statistical. Chicago: Fergus Printing Co., 1892.

Illustrated Historical Atlas of Randolph County, Illinois. W. R. Brink & Co., 1875.

"The Importance of Steamboats." *Journal of the Illinois State Historical Society* 47 (1954): 426–28. Originally published in the *Galena Gazette,* 9 December 1837.

Index to the 1850 Census of Randolph County, Illinois. Yakima, Wash.: Yakima Valley Genealogical Society, 1976.

"Is It Scriptural: Instrumental Music in Religious Worship." *Reformed Presbyterian Witness and Missionary Advocate* (February 1902): 41–44.

Jensen, Richard J. *Illinois: A Bicentennial History.* New York: W. W. Norton & Co., Inc., 1978.

Johnson, Allen, ed. *Dictionary of American Biography.* New York: Charles Scribner's Sons, 1927.

Johnston Family Bible. Owned by Mrs. Russel Hayes, Sparta, Ill.

John Worth v. William Hayes, 1841–1847. Randolph County Circuit Court. Record Book B. Randolph County Courthouse, Chester, Ill.

Koerner, Gustave. *Memoirs of Gustave Koerner, 1809–1896.* Cedar Rapids, Iowa: Torch Press, 1909.

Lippincott, Peter, ed. *Psalm Singing of the Covenanters.* University City, Mo.: Prairie Schooner Records, 1977.

Matthew Chambers v. The People of the State of Illinois. In *Reports of Cases Argued and Determined in the Supreme Court of the State of Illinois,* by J. Young Scammon, 351–360. Chicago: Callaghan & Co., 1886.

McGregor, Jean. *Chronicles of Saratoga.* Saratoga Springs, N.Y.: Bradshaw Printing Co., 1947.

Montague, E. J. *A Directory, Business Mirror, and Historical Sketches of Randolph County.* Alton, Ill.: Courier Steam Book & Job Printing House, 1859.

Muelder, Hermann R. *Fighters for Freedom: A History of Anti-Slavery Activities of Men and Women Associated with Knox College.* New York: Columbia University Press, 1959.

————. "Galesburg: Hot-Bed of Abolitionism." *Journal of the Illinois State Historical Society* 38 (September 1942): 216–35.

Nebelsick, Alvin Louis. *A History of Belleville.* Belleville, Ill.: Township High School & Junior College, 1951.

Park, Siyoung. "Land Speculation in Western Illinois Pike County, 1821–1835." *Journal of the Illinois State Historical Society* 77 (1984): 115–28.

Pease, Theodore Calvin. *The Frontier State, 1818–1848.* Urbana: University of Illinois Press, 1918.

Peck, J. M. *A Gazetteer of Illinois in Three Parts.* Philadelphia: Grigg & Elliot, 1837.

The People v. Matthew Chambers. Randolph County Circuit Court, Record Book B. Randolph County Courthouse, Chester, Ill.

The People v. William Hayes and Daniel Morrison, 1846. Clinton County Circuit Court. Record Book C. Clinton County Courthouse, Carlyle, Ill.

Perry County, Illinois, 1850 Census. Comp. Maxine E. Wormer. Thomson, Ill.: Heritage House, 1973.

"Petition for Slavery in Kaskaskia and Cahokia." *Journal of the Illinois State Historical Society* 47 (1954): 94–96.

Portrait and Biographical Record of Randolph, Jackson, Perry, and Monroe Counties. Chicago: Biographical Publishing Co., 1894.

Quaife, Milo M. "The Significance of the Ordinance of 1787." *Journal of the Illinois State Historical Society* 30 (1937–1938): 415–28.

Randall, Ruth Painter. *The Courtship of Mr. Lincoln.* Boston: Little, Brown & Co., 1957.

Regan, John. *The Emigrant's Guide to the Western States of America; or Backwoods and Prairies.* 1852. Ann Arbor, Mich.: University Microfilms, 1978.

Sarah, alias Sarah Borders, a woman of color v. Andrew Borders. In *Reports of Cases Argued and Determined in the Supreme Court of the State of Illinois,* by J. Young Scammon, 341–351. Chicago: Callaghan & Co., 1886.

Scammon, J. Young. *Reports of Cases Argued and Determined in the Supreme Court of the State of Illinois.* Vol. 4. Chicago: Callaghan & Co., 1886.

Siebert, Wilbur H. *The Underground Railroad from Slavery to Freedom.* 1898. New York: Arno Press, 1968.

Simon, Paul. *Freedom's Champion: Elijah Lovejoy.* Carbondale: Southern Illinois University Press, 1994.

Skeen, C. Edward. "'The Year Without a Summer': A Historical View." *Journal of the Early Republic 1* (Spring 1981): 51–67.

Smelser, Marshall. "Material Customs in the Territory of Illinois." *Journal of the Illinois State Historical Society* (April 1936): 5–41.

Sparta Democrat. Selected Articles, 1840–1841.

Sparta Herald. Selected Articles, 1840.

State of Illinois Archives Division Public Domain Sales Land Tract Record Listing. Springfield, Ill.

Sutton, Robert M. "Edward Coles and the Constitutional Crisis in Illinois, 1822–1824." *Illinois State Historic Journal* 82 (Spring 1989): 33–46.

Sylvester, Nathaniel. *History of Saratoga County, New York.* Philadelphia: Everts & Ensign, 1878.

Talkington, Laurie McCarthy. *The Illinois River: Working for Our State.* Champaign: State of Illinois Office of Publications Services, 1998.

Temple, Sunderine (Wilson), and Wayne C. Temple. *Illinois' Fifth Capitol.* Springfield, Ill.: Phillips Brothers Printers, 1988.

Tillson, Christiana Holmes. *A Woman's Story of Pioneer Illinois,* ed. Milo Milton Quaife. 1919. Carbondale: Southern Illinois University Press, 1980.

Torrens, Mrs. Frank. *Narratives of Randolph County.* Sparta Public Library, Sparta, Ill.

Townley, Wayne C. *Two Judges of Ottawa.* Carbondale: Egypt Book House, 1948.

Underwood, Larry. "The Passing of an Era." *Outdoor Illinois* (February 1975): 8.

Vos, J. G. *The Scottish Covenanters.* Pittsburgh: Crown & Covenant Publications, 1940, 1980.

Washburne, E. B. *Sketch of Edward Coles, Second Governor of Illinois and of the Slavery Struggle of 1823–24.* 1882. New York: Negro Universities Press, 1969.

Western Citizen. Selected Articles, 1842–1844.

White, Horace. *The Life of Lyman Trumbull.* Boston: Houghton Mifflin Co., 1913.

Whitney, Ellen M., comp. Janice A. Petterchak and Sandra M. Stark, eds. *Illinois History: An Annotated Bibliography.* Westport, Conn.: Greenwood Press, 1995.

Wilcox, David Ray. "The Reformed Presbyterian Church and the AntiSlavery Movement." Ph.D. diss. Colorado State College of Education at Greeley, 1948.

William Hay{e}s v. Andrew Borders. In *Reports of Cases Argued and Determined in the Supreme Court of the State of Illinois,* by Charles Gilman, 1:46–69. Chicago: Callaghan & Co., 1886.

Wilson, Charles M. "The Year Without a Summer." *American History Illustrated* (June 5, 1970): 24–29.

INDEX

Carol Pirtle holds a bachelor's degree in English and history from Millikin University. A professional writer for many years, she has been awarded certificates of excellence from the Illinois State Historical Society for two of her books, *Shining Moments* and *Where Illinois Began: A Pictorial History of Randolph County*.

SHAWNEE BOOKS

Also available in this series . . .